Red Tie, Blue Tie

How To Tell Whether Someone is Liberal or Conservative in Any Possible Scenario

Gary M. Almeter
& Reese Cassard

First Printing: 2024
ISBN 978-1-954158-31-3

Humorist Books is an imprint of *Weekly Humorist* owned and operated by Humorist Media LLC.

Weekly Humorist is a weekly humor publication, subscribe online at weeklyhumorist.com

99 Wall Street New York, NY 10005

weeklyhumorist.com - humoristbooks.com - humoristmedia.com

**HUMORIST
BOOKS**
New York

We dedicate this book to Cricket. If there's anything liberals and conservatives can still agree on, it's that killing puppies is bad.

Table of Contents

INTRODUCTION

Here's a fun game: Drink every time you hear the phrase "We live in a divided country." You'll be in the ER by dinner. Like we said, fun! Jokes aside, the state of our union is contentious in good years and belligerent in election years. Resentment between iconoclast liberals and traditional conservatives is at a boil, and with Donald Trump perpetually on the ballot it feels as though the future of democracy itself is at stake. That's why we as writers, best friends, and citizens came together to ask the most American question of all: How can we profit off this?

Consider Red Tie Blue Tie our formal contribution to the culture wars. Is it a book full of jokes? Yes. Is it important? Maybe. After all, there's a good reason schools are named after Francis Scott Key instead of the soldiers who actually fought to defend Ft. McHenry. Words have power, and we're using ours to illuminate the inconvenient truth that everything you do—the clothes you wear, the cars you drive, the meals you eat and music you listen to, everything—can and will be perceived as a political statement. It's absurd and depressing and exhausting, but it's a part of life that you can either embrace or dedicate your life to changing. Like the atom bomb.

There are thousands of jokes in this book. Or there's one joke told thousands of different ways. Depends how you look at it. Regardless, we just hope they lighten the mood in what's bound to be a brutal election season for both sides. We're all in this together (unfortunately) and it's better for everyone if we can all laugh about it. This whole endeavor is silly, but we put serious effort into ensuring neither group feels demonized. In fact, if this book sells a million copies, you'll be disgusted by how quickly our ideals and priorities change. So please, if you're ready to laugh about the aesthetics of political identity, grab a copy, gather your family (yes, even that uncle) and read it out loud.

Reese Cassard
Gary Almeter

Part One -

INTRODUCTION TO IDEOLOGICAL TAXONOMY

Frequently Asked Questions

Q: Who the fuck are you?

Gary

Reese

A: Great question! We ask ourselves that every morning. We are writers and best friends who met via email and bonded over writing jokes.

Q: Are you really best friends?
A: Yes.

Q: Do you ever fight?
A: No.

Q: When this book sells a million copies and becomes a movie, giving you both fame and fortune, do you think you'll fight then?

A: Yes.

Q: Who would win in a fight?

A: Gary

Q: Why?

A: He has dad strength.

Q: Who would win in a race?

A: If it's a marathon, Gary. If it's a sprint, Reese.

Q: What makes you think you can make such sweeping generalizations about Americans in so many scenarios?

A: What are you, our therapist? Just like how we never asked to be born, we never asked to be so perceptive, nor did we ask to channel those perceptions into a creative outlet that will only satisfy us if strangers think it's funny.

Q: What if we don't think your book is funny?

A: Read the next page.

Q: When will you write the sequel?

A: The aesthetics of political identity change dramatically every five years, so, 2029.

What to Do If You Think We're Wrong

Did we say Republicans wear Oakleys when you, a diehard Democrat, have been wearing Gas Cans for five years now? Are you the rare conservative who appreciates drag brunch? What's that, your conservative friends go with you? O.K. Sure. We believe you. Here's a handy list of actions you can take.

1. **Complain.** Complain to your friends about how these two white dudes from a comedy book don't understand your culture or your country at all. Tell your parents. Tell your kids. Tell the city council at the town hall. Tell literally everyone you know and anyone you see. It will make you feel better, and it may increase our sales, so we're all for it.

2. **Sue Us.** Go for it. There are dumber lawsuits out there. Be warned, though, Gary is a recovering lawyer; and he's ready to bust out his litigation skills like a retired karate master forced to defend an innocent citizen.

3. **Fight Us.** This is actually one of your better options, as neither of us have won a fight in our life and neither owns a single gun. We do, however, live very far from each other. Depending on where you live, you'd either have to take 2-3 flights or drive thousands of miles to hit each of us. Is that worth all that time and money? Maybe. We don't know how mad you are.

4. **Eat a Big Cup of Shaved Ice.** This always makes Reese feel better.

5. **Eat a Big Bowl of Ice Cream.** This always makes Gary feel better.

6. **Go For a Walk.** This one's a classic.

7. **Watch the 1981 Film *Ordinary People*.** This one's more of a curve ball, but it works. Trust us. There's a reason it won Best Picture at the 57th Academy Awards, and something about it just hits the heart in all the right ways. By the time you're done, you won't even remember why you were mad at us.

8. **Cry About It.** This is usually an insult (typically by conservatives, for the record) but we both love a good cry. If you read a list of the past

five things that we each cried about you'd probably be like, "What do you mean you cried over olive oil?" But it happens, and when it does, you feel better after. Always.

9. **Tell Our Employers.** Believe it or not, we don't write these jokes for a living. Not yet at least. You won't find our day jobs in this book, but it's probably not that hard. Especially because we don't have common names. Both our bosses receive hundreds of emails a day, though, so don't expect a response.

10. **Write Your Own Book.** Go for it. We fucking dare you. You can even write the exact same jokes as us but flip the words "liberal" and "conservative" every time. That would actually be pretty funny.

How to Tell Whether Someone is Liberal or Conservative Based on Their Car

Liberals drive Subarus and conservatives drive Chevys. Everyone knows this.

Tesla drivers used to be liberal but have become increasingly conservative, for obvious reasons. The Cybertruck is a Trump vote with wheels.

If someone drives a Kia Soul—which was designed and marketed to young, urban commuters but ended up becoming one of the best-selling vehicles among senior citizens—they are sufficiently liberal to have a "COEXIST" bumper sticker but are sufficiently conservative to have shut down several affordable housing projects in their hometown.

If someone drives a Kia Telluride, they have at least 4 kids and no time for politics. Unless they're driving their Kia Telluride in Telluride, CO, in which case they are conservative and have plenty of time to rally against estate taxes.

If someone drives a Jeep Wrangler, they are conservative.

If someone drives a Jeep Liberty, they are liberal.

If someone drives that Jeep truck (we don't even know what it's called, but it has that boxy front and cute little bed; you'd recognize it) they're going through a minor identity crisis. They used to be super liberal, like front of the crowd at every rally, but then they got a job with a 401k and started to see how much of their paycheck goes to taxes and have kind of dialed it back. They bought a truck because they wanted a bed for outdoor adventures but it's really only been used to help friends move and lug home goods from Target, and that makes them sad. They'll vote for Biden, but that'll probably be the last time they ever choose a Democrat.

If someone drives a Ford they're conservative. Unless it's a Ford Aerostar, then they're a liberal singer-songwriter playing at breweries around the Pacific Northwest under the stage name "Doomsday Picnic."

If someone drives a vintage VW Van, they've been liberal since the day they were released from the Stanford Prison Experiment. If they drive the new, electric VW Van, they're conservative and just sold their last startup for $85 million.

If a woman drives a Hyundai Ioniq, she is liberal and doesn't care if people think it's a Prius.

If a man drives a Hyundai Ioniq, he is liberal and says he doesn't care that everyone at work picks on him for it but deep down it does hurt his feelings.

If someone drives a Suzuki Esteem, they can drift in a parking lot better than most professional stuntmen.

If someone drives a Mazda Miata, they are a professional stuntman in their dreams but a terrible driver in reality.

If someone drives a Mercedes, they are conservative, and their name is on the door of the firm.

If someone drives a Lexus, they are conservative and will be named partner at the firm soon. They swear.

If someone drives an Audi A5, they are a liberal content creator and will pay it off when their next video goes viral. On God.

If someone drives an Aston Martin, they're more interested in British politics despite living in L.A. and growing up in Ohio.

If someone drives a baby blue "punch buggy," they will drive to the polling station with "It's Raining Men" on full blast before voting for Biden.

If someone drives a green Range Rover, they will drive that thing to the polling station in a "Love is Love" T-shirt before voting for Trump.

If someone drives a Mini Cooper, they are liberal and they have strong opinions on graphic design.

If someone drives a refurbished Ford Bronco, they are conservative and have strong opinions on barbecue.

If someone drives an 18-wheeler, they are liberal, listen to Joyce Carol Oates' extensive oeuvre on audiobook throughout their long shifts and are sick of everyone assuming they're conservative.

If someone rides a Harley Davidson, they're sick of everyone assuming they're conservative even though it's true.

If someone rides a Kawasaki Ninja, they're sick of everyone assuming they're going through a major identity crisis even though it's true.

If someone drives a wrecking ball machine, they're living most kids' dreams. We're jealous.

How to Tell Whether Someone is Liberal or Conservative on a First Date

If a man suggests meeting at a coffee shop, he's liberal.

If he suggests meeting at a cocktail bar, he's conservative.

If he suggests meeting at a hybrid coffee shop/cocktail bar, he'll just try to mirror your political views.

If a woman wears a puffer vest from The North Face, she's conservative.

If she wears a mohair cardigan, she's liberal.

If she wears a North Face puffer vest over a mohair cardigan, she's been flirting with socialism for a while but also just came off a complicated breakup with a man who described himself as a "beige nationalist."

If a man says the words "What I'd really like to do is paint," he's liberal for about a date and a half.

If a woman says, "That's when I decided it was IPO or nothing," she's conservative until the check arrives.

If anyone says, "My Substack / Etsy Shop / Podcast pays the bills," their parents pay their bills.

If a man interrupts you once, he's just excited and nervous. If he interrupts you twice, he's just a dick.

If he interrupts you to say that players on the US women's national team don't make as much money as players on the men's national team for purely economic reasons, he's conservative.

If he interrupts you to say that he thinks it's, like, sooooo fucked up that Ryan Gosling got an Oscar nomination for Barbie while Margot Robbie—who played freakin' Barbie!—didn't, he's liberal.

If a woman interrupts you to say anything, you're either dreaming or about to make one of the most out-of-pocket comments this bar has ever heard.

If a man asks you on a date and wants to split the tab, he doesn't deserve a second date.

If a woman asks you on a date and insists on splitting the tab, well - it's hard to say. Modern dating is tricky like that.

A Guide to Liberal and Conservative Colors

Republicans are red and Democrats are blue. Everyone knows this. But what about the other colors? There's a whole rainbow out there, and thanks to the corporate greed at Pantone, there are even more. Don't worry though; this handy guide will help you understand the full spectrum of political colors.

All shades of green are liberal. Even the forest green used in camouflage.

All shades of brown are conservative. Even the mocha found in lattes.

Black is the only politically neutral color. White is conservative, for a litany of reasons, unless being worn by a female candidate on election day or swearing in day. Khaki is the most conservative color in the world, followed by ivory.

Purple used to be one of the most conservative colors but is now one of the most liberal. There are two reasons for this. The first is that purple used to be the color of wealth and royalty because the berries used to dye garments purple were rare and therefore quite expensive. That all changed thanks to advancements in farming, transportation, and production throughout the 17th and 18th centuries. The second reason is Prince.

Most shades of yellow are conservative. Think bumblebee yellow sports cars, pastel yellow Polo shorts, and bright yellow Tory Burch dresses. The only exception is the yellow used on the cover of the "For Dummies" books, which are essentially an alternate form of public education.

Peach Fuzz, Pantone's Color of the Year 2024, is extremely liberal. In fact, since introducing Color of the Year in 2010, the only conservative colors chosen by Pantone have been Tangerine Tango (2012) and Illuminating (2021).

Orange becomes more conservative every year. We know what you're thinking: "It's because of Trump, isn't it?" Wrong. It's because Americans are increasingly embracing DIY projects, making Home Depot (a safe space for conservatives) and their ubiquitous orange buckets more popular than ever.

Pink is the hardest color to pin down. Sometimes it's loud and liberal, like at the International Women's March. Sometimes it's quiet and conservative, like carnations outside the homes in rich neighborhoods. Anyone over 10 should be careful working pink into their wardrobe or home. You never know what kind of statement you're making.

Silver is liberal and gold is conservative. This one is because of Trump.

How to Tell if Someone is Liberal or Conservative on Spotify

If someone thinks boygenius is a podcast about *Doogie Howser*, that person is conservative.

If someone thinks Destiny's Child is the name of Wolfgang Amadeus Mozart's[1] first album, that person is a conservative with a touch of free-market anarchy in them.

If someone thinks the Smiths are the people down the street with whom your parents go to dinner now and again, that person is a conservative and periodically flirts with despotic neo-feudalism.

If someone gets Bruce Springsteen and Rick Springfield confused, that person is human.

If someone thinks the Arctic Monkeys is Aztec Camera, that person is a conservative Stalinist.

If someone thinks Aztec Camera is the Arctic Monkeys, that person is a liberal Trotskyist.

If someone thinks Luke Bryan and Zach Bryan and Zac Brown are all the same person, that person is a post-colonial plutocratic liberal. And a liberal. Obviously.

If someone has a playlist called "The Kennys" and it only contains songs by Kennys Chesney, Loggins, Rogers, and G, that person is a conservative cyber-utopianist. Obviously.

---

1   Wolfgang Amadeus Mozart was a prodigious talent, manifesting his musical genius at an incredibly tender age. By the time he was merely five years old, Mozart was proficient in playing multiple instruments. His first known compositions, written in 1761 when he was just eight, include Andante (K. 1a) and Allegro in C major (K. 1b). These early works already showcased his innate understanding of melody and harmony, hinting at the extraordinary body of work that was to follow. Mozart's early start in composition set the stage for a prolific career that would leave an indelible mark on classical music. His ability to create complex compositions at such a young age continues to astonish and inspire, serving as a testament to his unparalleled musical genius and creativity. Mozart was a liberal because he composed operas that broke societal norms, used innovative musical structures, and constantly pushed the boundaries of classical music. Plus, his fondness for lavish parties and his rebellious spirit clearly showed he was all about living life in a major key!

If someone finds it ironic that Keith Urban is a country singer while Jesse Rural is a hip-hop artist, that person is a liberal with just a tinge of the Eco-Hegelist in them.

If someone willingly chooses to believe that singer, songwriter, pianist, and producer Alicia Keys is Alicia Keys's real name and not a professional alias, that person is a whig.

If someone is sort of into Coldplay, that person is a liberal sometimes and a conservative sometimes and also a progressive egalitarianist most of the time.

If anyone wonders why Bob Dylan, Bob Seger, and Bob Marley are just Bobs while Bobby McFerrin, Bobby Darin, and Bobby Brown are Bobbys, and Robert Plant, Robert Palmer, and Robert Smith elected to stay Roberts, that person is a pan-Constitutional populist with just a whisper of Byzantinism and a tinge of Scandinavian ecoauthoritariansim informed by a smattering of Fitzhughisms.

Speaking of Bob Seger, if someone doesn't put Bob Seger's "Turn the Page" (the Live in Detroit 1975 version, obviously)[2] on every road trip playlist, then

---

2   Bob Seger's "Turn the Page," originally released in 1972, is a poignant exploration of the itinerant lifestyle of musicians, encapsulating themes of alienation, the quest for identity, and the dichotomy between public perception and private reality. Seger's reflective narrative also transcends the specific experiences of touring musicians to touch on broader human conditions. The song's opening with a melancholic saxophone sets a somber tone, immediately immersing the listener into the introspective journey of the protagonist. Seger's lyrical prowess is evident in his vivid portrayal of the physical and emotional toll of life on the road. The recurring motif of "On a long and lonesome highway, east of Omaha" not only situates the narrative geographically but also symbolizes the endless, solitary journey not just through space, but through life's trials and tribulations.

Central to the song is the theme of alienation. The musician, despite being surrounded by crowds and adulation, experiences profound isolation. Seger articulates this through powerful imagery, such as "You can listen to the engine moaning out its one-note song," where the engine's monotonous drone mirrors the protagonist's internal sense of detachment and monotony. This alienation is further exacerbated by societal misunderstandings and judgments, as depicted in the encounters with truck drivers and the feelings of being an outsider looking in on a world that doesn't understand or welcome him.

Moreover, "Turn the Page" delves into the theme of identity and the dichotomy between the public and private selves. The line "Here I am, on the road again; there I am, up on the stage" juxtaposes the transient, lonely existence on the road with the ephemeral moments of connection and purpose found in performance. This duality reflects the existential search for self amidst the facades required by professional and public life, a theme that resonates beyond the realm of musicians to the human experience at large.

The song's refrain, "Turn the page," serves as a metaphor for resilience and the relentless push forward despite the weariness and isolation. It speaks to the human capacity to endure, to face the next chapter,

that is one person with whom we don't ever want to road trip. Speaking of Bob Seger again, if someone tries to substitute "Turn the Page" on their ersatz "road trip playlist" with one of its progeny[3] to try to get us to go on the road

whatever it may hold, in the continuous search for meaning and belonging. The song encapsulates a profound narrative of existential reflection, articulated through the lens of a musician's life on the road. The themes of alienation, identity, and the dichotomy between public perception and private reality, underscored by Seger's emotive storytelling and evocative imagery, render the song a timeless reflection on the human condition and a staple of every road trip playlist.

Also, Bob Seger is from Detroit. And with Michigan poised to swing the 2024 election, we're appealing to every single Michigan votr with their very own footnote.

3   Songs that share similar themes with Bob Seger's "Turn the Page," particularly those exploring the nuances of life on the road, the loneliness of touring, the complexities of fame, and the dichotomy between public persona and private identity, but which are decidedly not Bob Seger's "Turn the Page" include:

"The Load-Out" by Jackson Browne. (This song delves into the life of musicians after a concert ends, highlighting the dichotomy between the energy of live performances and the quiet, often solitary work that comes after. It touches on themes of the transient lifestyle of musicians and the deep connection to music that sustains them), "On the Road Again" by Willie Nelson. (This classic country song celebrates the nomadic lifestyle of musicians, expressing the joy and freedom found in making music and moving from place to place. Despite its more upbeat tone, it also hints at the sacrifices and loneliness inherent in a life spent on the road), "Home" by Michael Bublé. (Contrasting with the more romanticized aspects of touring, this song captures the longing for home, stability, and loved ones that touring artists often experience. It reflects on the personal costs of a public career and the universal desire for belonging and comfort), "Running on Empty" by Jackson Browne. (Another entry by Jackson Browne, this song metaphorically uses the road as a backdrop for life's journey, touching on themes of exhaustion, the search for meaning, and the relentless passage of time amidst a life lived in the fast lane.) "Wish You Were Here" by Pink Floyd. (While not solely about the life of musicians, this song captures the feeling of alienation and disconnection, themes prevalent in "Turn the Page." It reflects on the distance between the self and others, both physically and emotionally, resonating with the loneliness and introspection of life on the road), "Hotel California" by The Eagles. (This iconic song explores themes of excess, illusion, and the often disorienting lifestyle of the rich and famous, with a narrative that can metaphorically apply to the music industry. It delves into the darker side of the Californian dream and the music industry's traps, echoing the alienation and identity crisis explored in "Turn the Page"), "Faithfully" by Journey. (This power ballad expresses the challenges of maintaining relationships and family life amidst the demands of touring. It highlights the personal sacrifices made by touring musicians and the commitment required to sustain love and connection from afar), "Life on the Road" by The Kinks. (This track from their concept album "Soap Opera" explores the monotony and isolation of touring life, highlighting the disconnection from normal life and the weariness that comes with constant travel), "Tour Song" by Jawbreaker. (This punk anthem speaks directly to the experiences of a touring band, touching on the excitement and novelty as well as the loneliness and longing for home and stability). "Ramble On" by Led Zeppelin. (Inspired by the works of J.R.R. Tolkien, this song, while more metaphorical, encapsulates the theme of a continuous journey and the quest for home and belonging, which can be likened to the touring musician's life). "Tired of Being Alone" by Al Green. (While not specifically about life on the road, this soulful ballad captures the essence of loneliness and longing for companionship, themes that are often felt by artists separated from loved ones during tours,) "Fast Car" by Tracy Chapman. (Although it's more about escaping problems and seeking a better life, "Fast Car" captures the sense of constant movement and the pursuit of something elusive that often accompanies life on the road. Also, if Tracy Chapman and Luke Combs can sing in harmony at the Grammys, we

trip with them, we will just scoff.

Speaking of Bob Seger yet again (or at least Bob Seger adjacent) if anyone throws Rascal Flatts's "Life is a Highway" on any old playlist and thinks that its presence alone makes the playlist a road trip playlist, we will literally run that person off the fucking road and into the fucking ditch while we are on our book tour promoting this very book.[4]

---

should all be able to sing in harmony), "This Life" by Vampire Weekend. (This song reflects on the complications and moral quandaries that come with a life lived in constant motion, including the toll it takes on personal relationships and the quest for meaning amidst it all), "Leaving on a Jet Plane" by John Denver. (This classic folk song beautifully encapsulates the feelings of departure and the pain of saying goodbye to loved ones, a common experience for those whose careers keep them on the move), "Movin' Out (Anthony's Song)" by Billy Joel. (While focused on the working-class desire to break free from a life of toil, this song also speaks to the broader theme of seeking change and the uncertainties and sacrifices that come with it, akin to the life of a touring musician.). While these songs, spanning various genres and eras, further enrich the narrative of the emotional and psychological landscape navigated by those who spend their lives in transit, be it for music, love, or the search for a better life, they are no substitute for the Seger classic.

4   Firstly, In the pantheon of road trip anthems, Bob Seger's "Turn the Page" stands in stark contrast to Rascal Flatt's rendition of "Life is a Highway," not merely in tonal quality but in the depth of narrative and emotional resonance, making it a superior choice for a road trip playlist. Seger's specimen, with its haunting saxophone intro and gravelly vocals, encapsulates the solitary introspection and existential musings that often accompany long drives. The song's lyrical profundity, exploring themes of alienation, the dichotomy of public and private personas, and the relentless passage of time, invites listeners into a reflective journey, mirroring the physical journey of a road trip. Conversely, "Life is a Highway," while infectious and upbeat, offers a more surface-level engagement with the concept of travel, focusing on the exhilaration of the open road and the promise of adventure. Its pop-country sensibility and

If someone's Spotify Wrapped for 2021 skews a little melancholy, that is okay. It was literally 2021. But also, it's okay to not be okay. For example, Gary's most played Spotify song in playlist a road trip playlist, we will literally run that person off the fucking road and into the fucking ditch while we are on our book tour promoting this very book.

If someone's Spotify Wrapped for 2021 skews a little melancholy, that is okay. It was literally 2021. But also, it's okay to not be okay.[5] For example,

---

catchy chorus make it an accessible and immediate anthem, yet it lacks the layered complexity and emotional depth found in "Turn the Page." Seger's ability to evoke a poignant sense of both the freedom and isolation of the road offers a richer, more contemplative backdrop to a journey, making it a more fitting and rewarding companion for the introspective nature of long drives. Secondly, in the discourse of musical curation, particularly concerning the creation of road trip playlists, the inclusion of Rascal Flatts's "Life is a Highway" does not, by itself, confer upon a playlist the quintessential qualities required for such a categorization. This assertion is grounded in the multifaceted nature of road trip playlists, which necessitate a harmonious blend of thematic relevance, emotional diversity, and narrative depth to complement and enhance the journey's experiential tapestry. As discussed, "Life is a Highway" is characterized by its upbeat tempo and anthemic chorus, themes that undeniably resonate with the spirit of travel and adventure. However, the essence of a road trip playlist extends beyond the superficial allure of movement and exploration encapsulated in this single track. A truly representative road trip playlist demands a careful selection of songs that mirror the vast array of human emotions and experiences encountered along the journey—songs that evoke introspection, joy, melancholy, and a sense of wanderlust. The monothematic focus of "Life is a Highway," to wit, the euphoric aspects of travel overlooks the nuanced emotional landscape of a road trip, which can include moments of solitude, reflection, and even existential questioning, often evoked by the changing landscapes and the passage of time. The road trip experience, with its inherent fluctuations in mood and scenery, requires a soundtrack that can adapt and respond to these shifts, providing a backdrop that is both reflective and anticipatory. Furthermore, the depth of a road trip playlist is enhanced by lyrical and musical diversity, which allows for a more profound engagement with the journey. The inclusion of songs from various genres, eras, and cultural backgrounds can enrich the travel experience, offering a panoramic view of the human condition through the lens of music. In conclusion, while "Life is a Highway" may capture the exhilarating aspect of travel, its singular narrative and emotional tone fall short of encapsulating the complex tapestry of a road trip, thereby rendering it insufficient as the sole determinant of a road trip playlist.

Also, Rascal Flatts is from Tennssee, a state which has, since WW2 and with the exception of the Clinton/Gore years, been red. So no need to appease them.

5   In the swirling vortex of existential ponderings, the adage "it's okay to not be okay" serves as a beacon of solace, illuminating the murky waters of human tribulation. This philosophical nugget, while comforting in its embrace of life's tumultuous ebbs and flows, paradoxically coexists with the superior tranquility inherent in the state of being "OK." To unravel this conundrum, one must embark on a metaphysical jaunt through the labyrinth of emotional well-being. The acknowledgment that one's current state of not being OK is, in itself, an acceptable facet of the human experience, offers a peculiar sort of liberation. It's akin to dancing in the rain with leaky boots; the water seeps in, but the joy of the dance overshadows the discomfort. However, ascending from this quagmire to the serene plateau of OK-ness is akin to donning a pair of impermeable galoshes; the dance continues, unmarred by the intrusion of damp socks. Ergo, the journey from not OK to OK is not a linear progression but a whimsical frolic through a spectrum of emotional hues. It is in this dance - sometimes with leaky boots, sometimes with

Gary's most played Spotify song in 2021 was Lucy Dacus's "Thumbs." Reese's was "Uptown Funk" by Mark Ronson (featuring Bruno Mars) but Reese is anomalous in so many respects. His second most-played song in 2021, "Driver's License" by Olivia Rodrigo which tracks. Though his third most-played song of 2021 was "I Gotta Feeling" by the Black Eyed Peas. That Reese!!

If someone puts R.E.M.'s "Everybody Hurts" on a sad playlist, that person is an oligarchical imperialist.

If someone thinks Sufjan Stevens's "Tonya Harding (In D Major)" is one of, if not the best songs about Tonya Harding, that person is a theocratic anti-revisionist.

If someone frequently wonders if anyone else has a favorite member of boygenius because they definitely do and they sometimes feel bad about it because it feels wrong to commoditize and categorize Phoebe, Julien, and Lucy in the same way that beauty pageants feel wrong, that person is a Freudo-Pinochetist.

---

galoshes - that the tapestry of life is woven. Thus, while it is acceptable to momentarily bask in the rain of not being okay, the pursuit of the dry warmth of OK-ness remains a commendable endeavor, enriching the dance of existence with a kaleidoscope of emotional textures.

How to Tell if Someone is Liberal or Conservative While Trying to Solve the JonBenét Ramsey Case

If someone thinks an unknown intruder is responsible for the murder of JonBenét, that person is a conservative.

If someone thinks both of JonBenét's parents are responsible for the murder, that person is a liberal.

If someone thinks JonBenét's brother Burke is responsible for the murder, that person is a patriarchal fundamentalist.

If someone thinks that someone who knew the Ramsey family personally, but they are not sure who is responsible for the murder, that person is a monarchist.

If someone thinks that Patsy Ramsey alone is responsible for JonBenét's murder, that person is a transnational radicalist.

If someone thinks a wolf broke into the home and ate JonBenet, that person is a Gandhian socialist.

If someone thinks one of John Ramsey's business rivals is responsible for the murder, that person is a revolutionary syndicalist (likely from the Budapest school of Revolutionary syndicalism).

If someone thinks Santa Claus impersonator, Billy McReynolds, who was at the family home just days before the murder, is responsible for the murder, that person is a post-political transhumanist.

If someone thinks that one of JonBenét's toddler beauty pageant rivals' moms is responsible for the murder, that person is a liberal and also an Otto von Bismarckist.

How to Tell if Someone is Liberal or Conservative by The Scent they Leave in Their Wake

Florals

Scent	Liberal or Conservative	Analysis
Rose	Conservative	Classic, symbolizes tradition
Lavender	Liberal	Soothing, advocates for calm and peace
Jasmine	Liberal	Exotic, embraces diversity and uniqueness
Lilac	Conservative	Nostalgic, holds onto memories of spring
Gardenia	Liberal	Opulent, enjoys the finer things in life
Peony	Liberal	Romantic, values beauty and tenderness
Cherry Blossom	Conservative	Delicate, appreciates the fleeting beauty of life
Violet	Liberal	Modest, finds beauty in simplicity
Orchid	Conservative	Elegant, values sophistication and rarity
Lily of the Valley	Liberal	Cheerful, symbolizes adoration and loyalty

Industrial

Scent	Liberal or Conservative	Analysis
Gasoline	Conservative	Powerful, associated with traditional energy sources
Fresh Paint	Liberal	Creative, symbolizes new beginnings and projects
Sawdust	Conservative	Earthy, appreciates the raw essence of craftsmanship
Leather	Conservative	Refined, values durability and heritage
Metal	Liberal	Innovative, drawn to the strength and potential of materials
Rubber	Conservative	Practical, values reliability and utility

Scent	Liberal or Conservative	Analysis
Asphalt	Liberal	Enduring, reflects the infrastructure of society
Chlorine	Conservative	Clean, values purity and meticulousness
New Car Smell	Liberal	Modern, embraces the conveniences of contemporary life
Solder	Conservative	Precise, admires meticulous skill and technique

Spices and Herbs

Scent	Liberal or Conservative	Analysis
Sage	Liberal	Warm, evokes a sense of comfort and nostalgia
Mint	Conservative	Refreshing, values clarity and freshness
Cardamom	Liberal	Vibrant, enjoys the zest of life and new experiences
Basil	Conservative	Sweet, finds solace in simple pleasures
Rosemary	Liberal	Robust, appreciates a strong foundation and memory
Lavender	Conservative	Calming, prefers a traditional touch of elegance
Ginger	Liberal	Zesty, embraces bold and adventurous flavors
Turmeric	Conservative	Earthy, grounded in tradition and health
Saffron	Liberal	Exotic, values rarity and a touch of luxury
Thyme	Conservative	Timeless, respects the enduring essence of tradition

Seasonal Scents

Scent	Liberal or Conservative	Analysis
Pumpkin Spice	Liberal	Evokes warmth and comfort, embraces change
Peppermint	Conservative	Crisp and traditional, a return to basics

Scent	Liberal or Conservative	Analysis
Fresh Pine	Conservative	Grounded in tradition, reminiscent of the holidays
Ocean Breeze	Liberal	Fresh, open to new adventures and possibilities
Autumn Leaves	Liberal	Reflective, embraces change with a nostalgic touch
Winter Frost	Conservative	Crisp, clear, appreciates the quiet of winter
Spring Rain	Liberal	Renewal, welcomes new beginnings with freshness
Summer Night	Liberal	Mysterious, embraces the warmth of shared stories
Cinnamon	Conservative	Spicy yet traditional, warms up to the familiar
Apple Cider	Liberal	Homely, cherishes shared moments and traditions

How to Tell Whether Someone is Liberal or Conservative at a Cookout

If the grill is charcoal, the host is conservative.

If the grill is gas, the host is liberal.

If the grill is a gas / charcoal hybrid, the host is a political hybrid, if you will.

If the grill master is wearing boat shoes, they are conservative and you're about to eat the worst burger of your life.

If the grill master is wearing Nike Air Monarchs, they are conservative and you're about to eat the best burger of your life.

If the grill master is wearing Birkenstocks, they are liberal and you're about to eat the worst Impossible Burger of your life.

If the grill master is wearing white half-calf socks and black slides, they are liberal and you're about to eat the best brisket of your life.

If the grill master is wearing an apron that says "Cassard's Ceremonial Colorado Chili Cookoff Champion" he is Reese's friend Austin. Shout out to Austin.

If a guest insists that they can't taste the difference between vegan beef and real beef, they're liberal. If a guest insists that they can tell and that real beef is better, they're conservative. Both of them are lying.

If a guest brings cornhole, they're conservative.

If they bring all the necessities for "Chicken Shit Bingo[6]," including the chicken, they are extremely conservative.

If they bring a tie-dye kit, they're liberal. Unless it's a kid's birthday party, then they're just trying their best.

If they bring all the necessities for balloon animals, you better be at a kid's birthday party. If you're not, leave. Immediately.

If someone says "Hold my beer" you're about to witness either the most or the least athletic feat in your life.

If someone says "Hold my sword," you're still at the adult balloon party cookout. Don't say we didn't warn you when it's time to eat.

---

6   Chicken Shit Bingo is a unique, rural gambling game often played in Texas and other Southern states. The game involves a chicken, a board marked with a grid of numbers, and players who bet on where the chicken will defecate. Each square on the grid is numbered, and participants buy tickets corresponding to these numbers. The chicken is then placed on the board, and the game concludes when the chicken excretes on a square. The person holding the ticket with the corresponding number wins a prize.

Chicken Shit Bingo is not just a quirky pastime but a cultural phenomenon that reflects the rural lifestyle and community spirit. It often takes place in informal, social settings like local bars or community fairs, fostering a sense of camaraderie among participants. The game's simplicity and the element of chance make it accessible and entertaining. Additionally, it serves as a fundraiser for local causes, demonstrating its social and economic relevance in rural communities.

How to Tell if Someone is Liberal or Conservative at the Zoo

Tired of going to the zoo and not knowing where the animals stand on hot button political issues?

Think that the penguins are really cute and fun but not sure if you should support them based on their position on climate change? Wondering how that giraffe balances humanitarian concerns and national security when it comes to immigration? Want to pet that rabbit in the petting zoo but not sure where

it stands on economic inequality and whether it has been calling for more equitable wealth distribution and social safety nets? See that monkey looking at you and wish you knew where it stood on questions about privacy, data security, and the ethical use of artificial intelligence? These topics not only dominate political discourse but also challenge us at the zoo.

One of Reese's talents (in addition to skiing, copywriting, and playing lacrosse) is talking to animals. This is what he's learned.

Reptiles

Animal	Liberal or Conservative	Analysis
Crocodile	Conservative	Sticks to traditional waterways. Native to Florida. Doesn't even read books.
Turtle	Conservative	Very slow to change. Thinks Mitch McConnell is sexy.
Snake	Conservative	Flexible but prefers not to show its true colors.
Iguana	Liberal	Enjoys a laid-back, sunny disposition.
Chameleon	Liberal	Changes colors, open to different perspectives.

Animal	Liberal or Conservative	Analysis
Gecko	Liberal	Small but open to exploring new environments.
Alligator	Conservative	Defends its territory with a conservative grip. Also native to Florida. Would give its skin to make Ron DeSantis a new pair of platform lift boots.
Komodo Dragon	Liberal	Dominant, forked tongue, advocate for national parks.
Tortoise	Conservative	Old soul, values the wisdom of age. Jerks its turtle cock or fingers its turtle vagina to Mitch McConnell.

Birds

Animal	Liberal or Conservative	Analysis
Eagle	Conservative	Proud, sticks to high perches of tradition. Is picytured on our money.
Parrot	Liberal	Vocal about a variety of issues, embraces diversity.
Owl	Liberal	Wise, likes books. Even banned ones.
Swan	Liberal	Graceful, values the beauty in diversity.
Falcon	Independent	RFK Jr. is a master falconer and trains these birds of prey, showcasing his dedication to preserving natural habitats and promoting ecological balance.
Pigeon	Liberal	Common, adapts well to urban environments. Hangs out in public places smoking cigarettes and eating tacos from taco trucks. Would love more taco trucks.
Canary	Conservative	Likes to hang out in the coal mine. Thinks coal is the future.
Cockatoo	Liberal	Flashy; has a bite force of 250-300 psi - strong enough to bite off a human finger.

Animal	Liberal or Conservative	Analysis
Sparrow	Conservative	"Are not two sparrows sold for a penny? Yet not one of them will fall to the ground outside your Father's care. And even the very hairs of your head are all numbered. So don't be afraid; you are worth more than many sparrows." *Matthew 10: 29-31*

Insects

Animal	Liberal or Conservative	Analysis
Butterfly	Liberal	Embraces transformation and beauty.
Bee	Liberal	Communal, works for the greater good.
Ant	Conservative	Structured, values order and hierarchy.
Ladybug	Liberal	Cheerful, brings luck to all.
Dragonfly	Conservative	Adaptable, masters of change.
Grasshopper	Liberal	Jumps at new opportunities, embraces change.
Spider	Conservative	Independent, sticks to its web of tradition.
Firefly	Liberal	Lights up the night, an icon of hope.
Cockroach	Conservative	Survivor, thrives in tough conditions. Super curious about nuclear apocalypse just to see if it will, like Cher, survive.
Mosquito	Conservative	Persistent, follows its own path.

The Farm

Animal	Liberal or Conservative	Analysis
Cow	Conservative	Content with the status quo, enjoys routine.
Pig	Liberal	Curious, enjoys muddying the waters.
Chicken	Conservative	Pecking order matters, values tradition.
Sheep	Conservative	Flocks together, wary of change.

Animal	Liberal or Conservative	Analysis
Goat	Liberal	Adventurous, climbs to new heights.
Horse	Liberal	Noble, strides towards progress.
Duck	Liberal	Fluid, adapts to both land and water.
Turkey	Conservative 	Traditional, associated with festivities. Relishes being the juicy centerpiece of the one day you have to sit next to your uncle who is Facebook friends with the Q-Anon Shaman of January 6.
Rabbit	Liberal	Hops into new opportunities, seeks adventure.
Donkey	Conservative	Sturdy, carries the weight of tradition.

Jolene

This iconic Dolly Parton song has sparked countless interpretations over the years, but one of the lesser-explored aspects is the political leaning of its titular character. With absolute certainty and drawing upon the rich tapestry of the song's lyrics, one can assert that Jolene was, indeed, a liberal at heart.

Firstly, consider the lines, "Your beauty is beyond compare / With flaming locks of auburn hair / With ivory skin and eyes of emerald green." Jolene's bold self-expression through her vibrant hair and unique style screams of a liberal ethos, embracing individuality and defying conventional norms. Moreover, Jolene's alleged ability to easily capture the attention of Dolly's man, despite being asked not to, could be seen as a manifestation of liberal values—championing freedom and personal choice, albeit controversially in the realm of romantic entanglements.

Jolene's global appeal, hinted at by the line, "I had to have this talk with you / My happiness depends on you," suggests a universal, inclusive approach, aligning more closely with liberal perspectives that prioritize empathy and interconnectedness. While some might argue that Jolene's actions disrupt traditional marital structures, suggesting a conservative rebellion against societal norms, the depth of emotion and open dialogue in the song lean more towards a liberal narrative of understanding and emotional expression.

Caroline

One might be inclined to assume that, in light of its pervasive use at liberal-bastion Boston's Fenway Park and supposed source of inspiration in Caroline Kennedy, that Caroline is liberal. However, should one venture to decode the political leanings of the song's muse through a more authoritative analysis of the lyrics. It's clear that Caroline is a conservative.

Consider the line, "Good times never seemed so good." This sense of nostalgia, a yearning for the simplicity and joy of bygone days, resonates deeply with conservative values that cherish tradition and the preservation of the past's golden moments. It's as if Caroline herself is a beacon of timeless values in an ever-changing world. It's as if she wants to make America... no. We won't say it.

The communal sing-along nature of "Sweet Caroline," particularly in the chorus, "Sweet Caroline, good times never seemed so good," suggests a strong– ersatz cloistered– sense of community and collective harmony, principles often celebrated in conservative circles. Caroline becomes a symbol of unity and shared joy, reinforcing social bonds that conservatives hold dear. Furthermore, the song's overall wholesome and uplifting vibe, devoid of any radical calls for change or rebellion, aligns with a conservative preference for stability and incremental evolution over radical upheaval. Caroline's sweet and reassuring presence in the song serves as a reminder of the comfort found in the familiar and the cherished.

Part Two -

DAY TO DAY BUSINESS

How to Tell Whether Someone is Liberal or Conservative at the Coffee Shop

If someone orders drip black, they're conservative.

If someone orders drip with oat milk, they're liberal.

If a woman orders a caramel macchiato and a small piece of chocolate, she's conservative.

If a man orders the same thing, he's liberal.

If anyone orders an iced coffee with extra cream to-go at 10:30 on a weekend, they're hungover.

If someone orders decaf, with or without cream, they're just buying something to use the WiFi.

If they're working on a MacBook with no stickers, they're conservative.

If they're working on a MacBook with stickers, they're liberal. Unless one of the stickers is Calvin pissing on the Mac logo. Then they're conservative.

If they're working on a screenplay, they're liberal.

If they're working on their citizen journalism blog, they're conservative.

If a man is working on a novel, he's conservative. If a woman is doing the same, she's liberal.

If a man is working on his political manifesto (it's always a man) he's probably conservative but he's definitely scary. Don't ask him about it. Don't even make eye contact.

If the female barista's T-shirt says "Don't Let the Cat Out or the Cops In," she's liberal. If it says "My Eyes Are Up Here," she's conservative. If it says "Starbucks™" she'll be fired if you find out her political opinions. Just give her a nice tip and enjoy your cappuccino.

If a woman is reading Joan Didion while drinking an americano and smoking an Elf Bar, she's liberal. And she's having a wonderful day. However, if she's doing the exact same thing but reading Sally Rooney, she's having a rough day.

If a man is reading Hunter S. Thompson while drinking from a French press and smoking a cigarette, he's conservative and will only have a good day if someone asks him what he thinks of the book so that he can say he actually prefers Tom Wolfe.

If someone orders a flat white they've never had a political opinion in their life.

How to Tell Whether Someone is Liberal or Conservative on the Sidelines of Your Kid's Soccer Game.

If parents bring Budweiser in a YETI cooler and drink them from red Solo cups, they're conservative.

If parents bring PBR in an RTIC cooler and drink them from the can but with koozies covering the label, they're liberal.

If parents bring Hamms in a Playmate and drink from the can with nothing hiding the label, they're actually the grandparents, and they just want to enjoy the day, and they're the most conservative people you'll ever meet.

If parents bring hard liquor, just keep an eye on them.

If someone shouts "Let's go Reagan!" they're conservative.

If they shout "Let's go Willow!" they're liberal.

If they shout "Let's go Brandon!" they won't always regret choosing that name, but they do right now.

If anyone's wearing Grateful Dead merch, they used to be liberal but are now conservative.

If anyone's wearing The Chicks merch, they used to be conservative but are now liberal.

If someone shouts "Open your eyes, ref! You're missing a great game!" they're conservative.

If someone shouts "How much are these 10-year-olds paying you?" they're liberal.

If someone shouts "FUCK YOU!" they're the parents who brought liquor earlier. We told you to keep your eye on them.

If the ref laughs, he's conservative.

If the ref cries, he's liberal.

If the ref stops the game and says "Jesus, Doug, how many times have I told you you're not welcome at these games? Your kids are in their twenties now, for Christ's sake!" he's usually liberal but he's about to embrace the conservative fantasy of vigilante justice.

If someone brings orange slices for not just the kids but the parents as well, they're the real MVP.

How to tell if Someone is Liberal or Conservative in Chipotle

If someone orders a burrito with black beans but insists on waiting until someone brings a fresh container of black beans to the line, that person is a conservative.

If someone tries to pay for their food with a GameStop gift card, that person is a liberal.

If someone orders "light beans" in their burrito and then clarifies that by "light beans" they mean a specific amount of beans and that specific amount is anywhere from 1-12, that person is a conservative.

If someone orders "light beans" in their burrito and then clarifies that by "light beans" they mean a specific amount of beans and that specific amount is anywhere from 13-24, that person is a liberal.

If someone thinks a burrito with > 24 beans still qualifies as "light beans," they are a liberal separatist.

If someone sharts in a Chipotle and leaves their chinos in the Chipotle bathroom, that person is a separatist liberal.

If someone sharts in a Chipotle and washes their chinos in the Chipotle bathroom, that person is a conservative.

If someone is in line at Chipotle behind a person who looks just like The Situation from MTV's Jersey Shore, and after The Situation look-alike gets their food that person yells, "Hey look everyone! It's The Situation," that person is a liberal.

If someone is in line at Chipotle behind a person looks just like The Situation from MTV's Jersey Shore, and after The Situation look-alike gets their food that person does not draw any attention to The Situation, that person is a conservative.

If someone orders their burrito quadruple wrapped, double every meat, double guac, white rice, both beans (three scoops each), all salsas, extra sour cream, and extra cheese, that person is liberal.

If someone walks into Chipotle and orders coffee, a hamburger, a cheeseburger, or french fries, that person is conservative.

If a person asks if the corn in the corn salsa is GMO-free but has the burrito artist put the corn in their burrito regardless of the answer, that person is a liberal.

How to tell if Someone is Liberal or Conservative at the Grocery Store

If someone refuses to use the self-checkout machine, that person is a conservative.

If a person quietly sings along when the grocery store PA system plays "Iris," the Goo Goo Dolls' 1998 hit from the City of Angels soundtrack while the person compares pasta shapes to identify the best substitute for ziti, that person is a liberal.

However, if that person loses their composure and loudly sings the "And I don't want the world to see me, 'cuz I don't think that they'd understand" part, that person is an anarcho-communist.

If a person quietly sings along when the grocery store PA system plays "Can't Hardly Wait," from the Replacements' 1987 album Pleased to Meet Me while the person stands over the deli counter contemplating the difference between lacy Swiss cheese and regular Swiss cheese, that person is a conservative.

If a person is stocking up on Lunchables, Cool Ranch Doritos, Funyuns, two-liter bottles of Mountain Dew, and Bagel Bites, that person is either a parent of several children they may or may not love or extremely high or both.

If a person tries to steal cabbage by stuffing it into their jacket, that person is a liberal.

If a person tries to steal cabbage by stuffing it into their purse, that person is a conservative.

If a person buys something obscure (like coconut flour, gin and tonic salmon, pumpkin spice gouda) and it doesn't scan at the checkout register and the person says, "well, looks like that item is free today!" then that person is a conservative.

If a person says, "It's real, I just made it this morning" when the cashier checks to see if their $20 bill is counterfeit, that person is a liberal.

How to Tell Whether Someone is Liberal or Conservative at the Park

If someone is walking in skinny jeans, they're conservative.

If someone is walking in baggy jeans, they're liberal.

If someone is walking in overalls, they're socialist.

If someone is walking in coveralls, they're either servicing the portable toilets or collecting signatures for a cause so liberal you'll struggle to believe it's not yet on a real ballot.

If a group of friends having a picnic is blasting Vampire Weekend from their Bluetooth speaker, they're liberal.

If they're blasting Luke Bryan, they're conservative.

If they're blasting Paul Simon or Goth Babe, Reese will ask to join.

If they're blasting Fleetwood Mac or The National, Gary will ask to join.

If two friends are passing a football 10 to 20 yards, one is liberal and the other is conservative. If they're tossing the ball 30 to 50 yards, both are conservative. If they're tossing it 50+ yards, one of them may be Brett Favre.

If a mother is pushing her child in a stroller with wheels originally designed for the battlefield in Desert Storm, she's conservative.

If she's carrying her child on an e-bike with tires fatter than a Harley Davidson's, she's liberal.

If someone is roller skating, they're liberal.

If they're rollerblading, they're conservative.

If they're skateboarding, they're whatever their parents aren't.

If they're unicycling, slacklining, or hula-hooping, they are liberal and they want you to give it a try. It's not that hard, they swear!

If they're cranking out pull-ups on the jungle gym, they're conservative and they want you to leave them alone. Don't even look.

If they're carrying a full-sized American flag and it's not one of the patriotic holidays, don't worry, they'll let you know where they stand politically whether you want to know or not.

How to Tell Whether Someone is Liberal or Conservative at a Bookstore

If a man lingers at the history section, he's conservative. Even if he's holding a JFK biography.

If a woman lingers in the sports section, she's liberal. Even if she's holding a Curt Schilling biography.

If a man is carrying a large stack of feminist fiction—classic or contemporary— he's liberal but not as liberal as he wants women to think he is. Expect to see him chain-reading all of them outside the coffee shop next door.

If a man is carrying a large stack of Ted Hughes poems, he is conservative and wants you to know it. Expect him to feature them prominently throughout his apartment.

If a woman is carrying a large stack of hard-boiled detective novels, there's a 75% chance she's conservative and a 3% chance she's plotting to murder her husband.

If anyone is carrying a large stack of classic sci-fi titles, they aren't very political and they haven't voted for a winning presidential candidate in 25 years.

If someone in tattered clothes is reading Proust with fingerless gloves during work hours, they are not experiencing homelessness. In fact, their trust fund won't run out for at least 10 more years.

If someone is reading *Atlas Shrugged,* they're the type of Libertarian that hates poor people.

If someone is reading *Tough Guys Don't Dance,* they're the type of Libertarian that hates women.

If someone is reading *Portnoy's Complaint,* they're the type of Libertarian that hates themselves.

If someone is perusing the beautiful hardcover art books, they're shopping for a housewarming gift. Don't ask for their opinion on Dali.

If someone is perusing the dusty old art history books, they're shopping for a new purpose in life. Don't ask for their opinion on Dali.

If a young woman is sliding across the shelves on the top rung of a rolling ladder, she is the heroine of a Netflix movie about someone rebuking the family business in favor of a career as a novelist. No one believes in her talent, but in five years (one hour on screen) her first novel will become a bestseller. Also, she's unapologetically liberal.

If an old man is sliding across the shelves on the top rung of a rolling ladder, he is the hero of a Netflix movie about someone refusing to sell the small business his father started in 1949 to a team of greedy real estate tycoons. No one shops at his bookstore anymore, but he doesn't care. Also, he's unapologetically conservative.

If a little kid gets lost in the sexuality section, they will either live in a commune or a rectory when they grow up.

If a little kid gets lost in the humor section, they will live in a studio apartment with roommates until they turn 45.

If anyone is seen buying this book, they have great taste.

How to Tell Whether Someone Is Liberal or Conservative at a Dive Bar

If someone orders Miller High Life, they're liberal.

If they order Labatt Blue, they're conservative.

If they order Genesee Cream Ale, they fill out their ballot from the bar, and they always write in their own candidate. This year: Elmer Fudd.

If a man at the pool table is wearing a mechanics shirt with a trucker hat, mullet, and a full sleeve of tattoos, he's either a trendy liberal or a classic conservative. There is no middle ground, but there is an easy way to find out where they stand: Ask them to help jump start your car. If they know how to do it, they're conservative. If they don't, they're liberal, and you should remind them that other cultures (blue collar workers) are not costumes.

If the woman at the pinball machine already has the high score, she's conservative.

If anyone plays anything by Elvis on the jukebox, they're conservative.

If anyone plays anything by Paul Simon on the jukebox, they're liberal.

If anyone plays "Sweet Caroline" on the jukebox, they ran out of ideas before quarters.

If a man is wearing more than one ring, he's liberal. Unless one is a wedding band and the other is a state championship ring from '76. Then he's a conservative who would have gone pro if he didn't blow out his knee at Tech freshman year.

If the bartender slides someone a beer the full length of the bar, he's neither liberal nor conservative. He's an actor in a beer commercial that's desperately trying to appeal to both demographics.

If someone smokes Marlboro Reds, they're conservative.

If someone smokes American Spirts, they're liberal, but they've already mentioned that, haven't they?

If a woman you've been talking to all night asks to bum a cigarette and then disappears with the whole pack, that's God telling you to quit.

If a couple in matching fedoras buys you a drink, they're about to make a very liberal proposition. Do what you will, though. We don't judge.

How to Tell Whether Someone is Liberal or Conservative at a Fancy Bar

If a man orders an old fashioned, he's conservative. If he orders a Negroni, he's liberal.

If a woman orders a dirty martini, she's liberal. If she orders a dry one, she's conservative.

If anyone orders an espresso martini, they're just trying to fit in.

If a man is wearing a suit and tie, he's liberal. If he's wearing a suit with no tie, he's conservative.

If a man is wearing a turtleneck, be careful.

If a woman is wearing a turtleneck, run.

If a woman is wearing a black leather jacket from Yves Saint Laurent, she's liberal. If she's wearing a black leather jacket from Ralph Lauren, she's conservative. Either way, she does not want you to buy her a drink.

If a man is wearing a T-shirt with a gold chain over it, he's conservative. If the chain is tucked underneath, he's liberal. If you're female, they both want to buy you a drink.

If someone uses the flashlight on their phone to read the cocktail menu, they are your parents. And they're conservative.

If the bartender has a waxed mustache and tattoos that read "LOVE" and "MORE" on his knuckles, half his sentences start with "I'm a lifelong Democrat, but..."

If the couple sitting at the window was laughing but just went silent, someone just told a Biden joke.

If the couple sitting at the booth has been silent all night, someone made a mother-in-law joke on the ride over.

If someone asks the bartender which bathroom to use because they aren't used to gender-neutral ones, they're still your parents, and this bar is only making them more conservative.

If anyone orders a non-alcoholic beer, they're conservative. But if they order a mocktail, they're liberal.

If anyone complains that the place just gets worse every time they visit, maybe they should just stop visiting.

How to Tell if Someone is Conservative or Liberal While Smoking

If someone smokes Winstons, they are conservative.

If someone smokes Marlboro Lights, they are liberal.

If someone smokes cigars, they are conservative, unless they're smoking one of about a thousand H. Uppman petites they had imported from Cuba just before signing an embargo against Cuban imports and they're wearing Wayfarers and a wool and cashmere blend cable knit sweater over their shoulders, gabardine trousers, loafers, white Sperry deck shoes, and a blue three-button polo shirt, in which case they are a liberal, because that person is JFK.

If a person smokes a pipe and blows smoke rings and as those smoke rings rise they transform into the Obama logo, they are liberal.

If a couple has a dinner party, and the next morning when the kids wake up and come downstairs the kids examine the party detritus and discover a bunch of cigarette butts in half-full wine glasses, at least one burn hole in the sofa, and there are at least a dozen cigarette butts with metallic pink lipstick residue on them, that couple is conservative but their kids will grow up to be liberal.

If a person smokes a pipe filled with tobacco they grew themselves on a farm that's been in their family for generations, they are conservative.

If a person smokes a pipe filled with golden Jamaican kush, they are liberal.

If a person smokes Benson & Hedges, they are conservative, but the sort of conservative who navigates a complex inner landscape of conformity and familial loyalty. This individual might publicly champion traditional values, support conservative political figures, and partake in discussions that reflect a conservative viewpoint, yet their adherence often lacks personal conviction and is instead rooted in a deep-seated desire not to upset familial dynamics. Such a person usually grew up in a household where conservative ideologies were the norm, shaping much of their social and cultural environment. Their personal identity, interwoven with their family's expectations, has become a tapestry of inherited convictions rather than self-discovered beliefs. This often leads to internal conflicts, especially when exposed to diverse perspectives that resonate more with their personal experiences or unspoken beliefs. Their conservative stance is less about a heartfelt agreement with the principles themselves and more about maintaining peace at family gatherings, preserving parental approval, and upholding the family's social image. This dynamic can leave them feeling unfulfilled or insincere, as they navigate the delicate balance between authenticity and familial obligation.

If a person has several Smokey Robinson records on vinyl, they are liberal.

If a person's favorite rendition of "Smoke Gets in Your Eyes" is Barbra Streisand's and how can we even ask them that, they are liberal.

If a person's favorite song is "Roll Me Up and Smoke Me When I Die" by Willie Nelson, they are liberal. But if a person really wants their loved ones to roll them up and smoke them when they die, they are conservative.

If you have ever smoked a blunt in the White House bathroom with Snoop Dogg, you are liberal.

If someone lights their hand-rolled cigarettes with a monogrammed table top lighter, they are conservative.

If someone can play the opening chords of Deep Purple's "Smoke on the Water," they are liberal.

If someone has ever put the Smithereens's song "Cigarette" on a mixtape, they are conservative.

If a person started smoking when they were 16 because they started hanging out with a crowd that was all too willing to show them every gas station in town that wouldn't card them buying cigarettes and the person thought it was a stupid habit and never really bothered smoking beyond socially until high school wore on and they were in a very bad place mentally and no one at home was doing anything about it so they occasionally started having cigarettes before school to brace themselves for the day and then by sophomore year everything had gone to hell because their mom was sick and their stepdad couldn't connect emotionally to anyone and their little brothers were infuriating and their girlfriend had just left and they were in an unhealthy relationship with an older man and had been grounded for an entire year with no way of passing the school year and lo and behold they start buying their own packs and having a few more in the morning until one day at the end of high school they are smoking a pack a day and their mother has died, that person is conservative.

If a person starts smoking because their friend's ex-boyfriend had these delicious Orange Cream Camels that came in a tin, and fuck, they are still the best-tasting cigarette they ever smoked, and they figured if that tasted so damn good, cigarettes, in general, couldn't be that bad, that person is liberal.

How to Tell Whether Someone is Liberal or Conservative at the Dog Park

If a man at the dog park has a pit bull named Rex, he's conservative. If the pit bull is named Lex, he's liberal.

If a woman at the dog park has seven pit bulls, each one named after one of the seven dwarfs, she's liberal and she needs your help finding a forever home for each of them.

If a couple in matching Barbour jackets has a springer spaniel, ask them what they think about John Kerry. If they say he was a mediocre Secretary of State but still voted for him over Bush in 2004, they're liberal. If they ask you to leave them alone, they're conservative.

If a couple in matching cowboy hats has a Great Dane, ask them what they think of Willie Nelson. If they say he's one of the greatest living songwriters and should be held in the same regard as Bob Dylan, they're conservative. If they say they "He's cool, why?" they're liberal.

If anyone at the dog park has a border collie, they're liberal. Conservatives with border collies keep them on the farm, where they belong.

If anyone at the dog park has a German short-haired pointer, they're conservative.

If anyone at the dog park has a beagle writing on a typewriter, they're Charlie and or Sally Brown and you're at the dog park with Snoopy himself. Incredible. We're so jealous.

If anyone at the dog park has a Bernese Mountain Dog, they're probably liberal but definitely have whiskey in their Yeti tumbler.

If anyone at the dog park has a poodle, they're probably liberal but definitely have wine in their Yeti tumbler.

If anyone at the dog park has a Bernedoodle, they're probably a swing voter, definitely have a variety pack of craft beer in their Yeti cooler, and may even give you one if you ask nicely.

If anyone pulls up to the dog park with two Golden Retrievers in the back of their Ford F-150, they're conservative. If they pull up with the retrievers in the back of a restored 1982 Ford Bronco, they're liberal. If they pull up with the retrievers in the back of a topless Range Rover, they're models shooting for next summer's Ralph Lauren catalog.

If a man shows up with a litter of Golden Retriever puppies, he's just trying to pick up girls.

How to Tell Whether Someone is Liberal or Conservative at the Airport

If you're in PDX, everyone is liberal.

If you're in DFW, everyone is conservative.

If a woman at the Delta lounge has three necklaces and seven rings, she's conservative.

If a man at the Delta lounge has three necklaces and seven rings, he's liberal.

If a man is reading *Men's Health* at the gate, he's conservative. If he's reading *Harper's*, he's liberal. If he's reading *Harper's Bazaar*, he forgot to bring something to read and took the first thing he could find out of his wife's bag.

If a family of four or more is all wearing matching Nike sweatsuits, they're liberal.

If a family of four or more is all wearing matching Marvel sweatsuits, they're conservative.

If a couple is wearing Sambas, they're liberal. The more obscure the colorway, the more liberal they are.

If a couple is wearing Dunks, they're conservative. The more traditional the colorway, the more conservative they are.

If a couple is wearing sandals, gross.

If a couple is wearing loafers, it's hard to tell, but we appreciate anyone who wears slip-ons through security.

If someone's wearing an ironic T-shirt through security that says "THE ONLY GUNS I'M SMUGGLING ARE THESE ARMS" they're conservative. If the shirt says "SCAN ME DADDY," they're liberal. Either way, keep up the good work.

If you see a man sprinting through security at the Honolulu airport shouting "Beth! Wait!" you're an extra in a romantic comedy called *Kisses in Kauai.*

If you see two flight attendants sprint to each other before passionately kissing while Alicia Keys' "If I Ain't Go You" plays in the background, you're an extra in a romantic comedy titled *Love is Delayed*.

If you see a man with his phone clipped to his belt and a printed boarding pass protruding from his chest pocket, he's conservative.

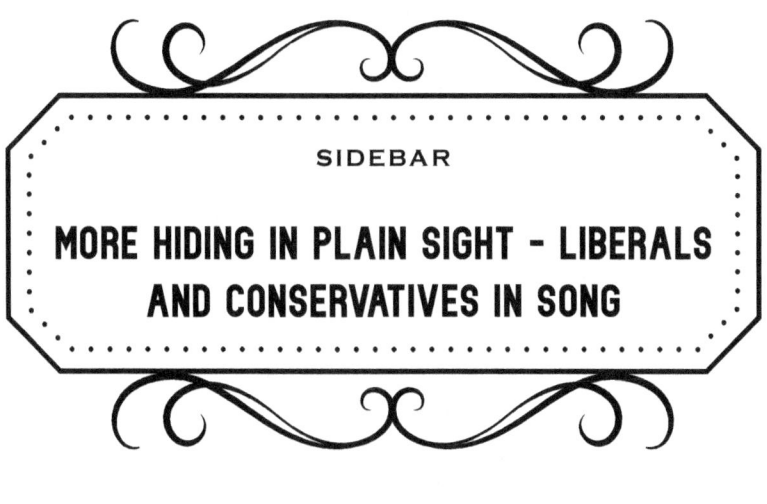

Angie

The Rolling Stones' haunting ballad paints a picture of heartache and longing and weaves a complex emotional tapestry that subtly hints at the title character's political inclinations. Our analysis reveals that Angie embodies a liberal spirit, characterized by her free-wheeling nature and the emotional depth of the song.

The Rolling Stones depict Angie as a figure of liberation and change, evident in the melancholic acceptance of a farewell: "Angie, you're beautiful, but ain't it time we said goodbye?" This willingness to embrace change, even when fraught with emotional pain, mirrors a liberal's readiness to accept the ebb and flow of life and the inevitable transformations that come with progress. The song's reflection on the tumultuous end of a relationship, coupled with the yearning for what might have been, suggests a depth of empathy and understanding. Angie's persona, entwined with these themes, resonates with liberal values that prioritize emotional intelligence, compassion, and an open heart toward the complexities of human connections. Moreover, the international allure of "Angie," with no explicit ties to a particular place or time, aligns with a liberal appreciation for universality and the shared human experience that transcends borders and ideologies.

Mandy

Barry Manilow's "Mandy" is a simultaneously poignant and rousing ballad that delves deeply into themes of love, loss, and reflection. Through the lens of this emotionally charged song, one finds that Mandy, the song's focal point, embodies a conservative essence, particularly in the context of her relationships and personal journey.

The lyrics, "Well, you came and you gave without taking, but I sent you away, oh Mandy," suggest a narrative of self-sacrifice and loyalty, qualities not unlike those of the American military and qualities revered in conservative ideologies. Mandy's willingness to give without taking resonates with traditional values of altruism and commitment, underpinning conservative views on personal responsibility and the importance of steadfastness in relationships. Moreover, the song's reflective tone, with its yearning for a past love and the somber acknowledgment of lost opportunities, aligns with a conservative nostalgia for what once was—a longing for the simplicity and purity of erstwhile connections, untainted by the complexities of the modern world.

Mandy's character, as portrayed through the emotionally laden verses, encapsulates the conservative ideal of unwavering devotion and the dignity in gracefully stepping away for the sake of one's beloved. Like how Newt Gingrich abandoned his lesbian sister. This narrative champions the virtues of honor and the timeless beauty of unrequited love, painting Mandy as a bastion of conservative romantic ideals.

Lucy

"Lucy in the Sky with Diamonds," the mesmerizing Beatles track, invites listeners into a kaleidoscopic world of vivid imagery and whimsical allure. Analyzing this enigmatic character, Lucy, through the prism of political ideology, leads one to the conclusion that she is a liberal.

Lucy, with her eyes of "kaleidoscope," guides us through a realm where "the girl with sun in her eyes" and "cellophane flowers of yellow and green towering over your head" reign supreme. This vibrant and surreal landscape, unfettered by conventional boundaries, mirrors the liberal penchant for embracing diversity, creativity, and the boundless exploration of ideas. Also drugs.

The song's celebration of imagination and the psychedelic tapestry it weaves can be seen as a metaphor for liberal values of open-mindedness and the rejection of rigid norms. Lucy, as the central figure in this dreamscape, personifies the liberal spirit's journey towards intellectual and cultural liberation. Also drugs.

Furthermore, the very nature of the song, with its abstract lyrics and speculative interpretations, aligns with the liberal inclination towards introspection and finding deeper meanings beyond the surface. Like when we are invited to "Picture yourself on a train in a station with plasticine porters with looking glass ties" it's like we are riding Amtrak from Wilmington, Delaware to Washington, DC on Joseph Robinette's Biden lap. Lucy, in her sky adorned with diamonds, becomes an icon of liberal thought, inviting us to look beyond the mundane and embrace a world brimming with possibilities and wonder.

Part Three -

SPORTS AND LEISURE

How to Tell Whether Someone is Liberal or Conservative in Co-ed Softball

If a man is playing in a Yankees cap and he's not from New York, he's liberal.

If he's wearing a Red Sox cap and he's not from Boston, he's conservative.

If he's wearing a Nationals cap and he's not from DC, he's playing on the National Mall because he read that participating in communal activities with your coworkers increases your chances for promotion.

If a woman is playing in Hokas, she's politically neutral.

If she's playing in soccer cleats, she's liberal and she will blush if you flirt with her.

If she's playing in softball cleats, she's conservative and she will slide into you spikes up if you flirt with her.

If the man playing shortstop wearing vintage track pants always makes the right play with the ball but is often late with the throw because his arm just doesn't have the juice it used to, he was conservative in college but has gotten more liberal with age.

If the man playing shortstop wearing a sleeveless hoodie occasionally makes the wrong play with the ball but always throws it with almost too much heat, he was born conservative and he will die conservative.

If a woman is playing shortstop, she just wants to play ball, man.

If a man contributes nothing but home runs at bat, he's conservative but you wouldn't know it right away.

If a man contributes nothing but beers in the dugout, he's conservative and you will know it immediately.

If a man contributes nothing but funny ideas for your team name, like "Raging Pitch" or "Pass the Bunt," he's liberal and wants you to subscribe to his election newsletter, "Heart & Poll."

If the woman in left field has small tattoos and a big arm, she's moving to France if Trump wins. She means it this time.

If the woman in center has big tattoos and a small strike zone, she's the team manager and has maintained high morale among her players for almost a decade now. We don't know what she is, but we would vote for her in any election.

If anyone bunts, under any circumstances, they're embarrassing themselves.

How to Tell If Someone is Liberal or Conservative in Pickup Basketball

If anyone is playing in a Punisher tee, they're conservative.

If anyone is playing in a Phish tee, they're liberal.

If a man is playing with a bandana as a headband, he's liberal.

If a woman is playing with a bandana as a headband, she's conservative.

If a man is playing in Jordan 11s, he's rich and liberal.

If a man is playing in Jordan 9s, he's rich and conservative.

If a man is playing in running shoes, he is liberal. Unless the shoes are grass-stained New Balances. Then he's conservative.

If a man is playing in Jordan 3s, baggy mesh shorts, and an even baggier pink polo, he's Adam Sandler.

If a man over 50 is playing in Chuck Taylors, he's probably conservative and probably the best player on the court.

If a man under 50 is playing in Chuck Taylors, he's definitely liberal and definitely the worst player on the court.

If a woman is playing in UGG boots, she's conservative. And a great three-point shooter. Draft her early.

If a man goes the whole game setting screens instead of shooting, he's liberal and fun to play with, but there's no need to use an early pick on him.

If anyone goes the whole game without passing, they are the worst. Avoid drafting them at all costs.

If a man is playing in rec specs, he's conservative. Unless that man is Naismith Hall of Fame center Kareem Abdul-Jabbar. Then he's very liberal.

If someone calls a foul because you had your hand on his hip when he went up to shoot even though he's been pulling your shirt all game, they're just an opportunist who pretends to be liberal around other liberals and then flips when the crowd changes. Give them the call either way. They'll probably miss anyways.

How to Tell Whether Someone is Liberal or Conservative at the Gym

If a man calls another man "chief," he's conservative. If he calls him "hoss," he's liberal.

If a woman is wearing a matching set from Lululemon, she's liberal. If the set is from Alo, she's conservative.

If a strong man is wearing a shirt with an AK-47 on it that reads "Come and Take It," he's conservative. However, if the man is scrawny, he's liberal and he's wearing it ironically.

If anyone over 50 is lifting in jeans, they are conservative. If anyone under 40 is doing the same, they are liberal. If they're in their 40s lifting in jeans, they're just at that hectic stage of parenthood where there's not even time to change between their kid's soccer practice and family dinner. They're too tired to have political opinions.

If anyone exclusively works out on the bench press or squat rack, they are conservative. If they exclusively work out in the designated HIIT area, they are liberal.

If a man asks someone to spot him but doesn't end up needing help, he's just showing off.

If a man's grunts sound like "Ahh Ahh Ahh" he's liberal. If they sound like "Urgh Urgh Urgh" he's conservative. If he lifts over 200 pounds without making a sound he's a dangerously unpredictable independent.

If anyone holds a plank for over five minutes they're so detached from the worries of the world that they can't tell you who the past three presidents were.

If a woman takes a picture flexing to the mirror by the free weights, she's conservative. If she throws up a peace sign, she's liberal.

If a personal trainer tells their client "the only thing holding you back is you," they're liberal. If they say "pain is weakness leaving the body" they're conservative. If they say "Oh yah! Vat is vat I'm talking about!!" They just moved here from Austria. Do not, under any circumstances, ask them what they think of American politics.

If anyone's wearing those shoes with the little spaces for each toe, they're conservative. You'd think it would be the opposite, but nope. Red as a tomato.

If a man is working out in a turtleneck, he's a Bond villain.

If a woman is working out in a sports bra that's dripping in sweat but her hair is still perfectly in place, she's a Bond girl.

If anyone is working out in Salomon Sportstyle sneakers, rent in your neighborhood is going up.

How to Tell If Someone is Liberal or Conservative While Playing Cornhole

Cornhole is a microcosm—and players will tell you it is the only microcosm that matters—of life. There are many distinct cornhole personas. Together, they weave a tapestry of political inclinations. You have to live the game to know. So put away your "clipboards" and your "statistics" and your "data" and your "whiteboard" and your "erasable markers" and your "pleated khakis," Steve Kornacki, and break out your beanbags and your boards.

The Archer. The Archer approaches each toss with the precision and focus of a medieval bowman. With a meticulously calculated stance and an unwavering gaze, this player draws the beanbag back as though nocking an arrow. The choice of a sleek, minimalist watch and the latest eco-friendly sneakers might hint at a liberal inclination, yet the focus and reverence for tradition suggest a conservative respect for the rules and rituals of the game.

The Flicker. Characterized by a nonchalant flick of the wrist, The Flicker embodies a laissez-faire approach to cornhole. This player's laid-back demeanor, often accompanied by a vintage band T-shirt and worn-in jeans, hints at a liberal ethos, embracing diversity and fluidity in both play and life. The Flicker's casual disregard for precision belies a deeper belief in inclusivity and the joy of participation over the rigidity of competition.

The Drove My Chevy to the Levy When the Levy was Dry Dickface. This player stops cornhole play whenever "their" song comes on the Bose outdoor speakers so they can dance, frolic about, and generally annoy everyone.

The Flinger. With a dramatic wind-up and a release that borders on the theatrical, The Flinger turns each toss into a performance. This player's flamboyant style, complete with brightly colored attire and perhaps an avant-garde hairstyle, suggests a liberal openness to self-expression and a rejection of conventional norms. The Flinger's penchant for making a statement, both in play and in appearance, mirrors the progressive drive for visibility and change.

Pythagoras. This player uses mathematical tenets to determine their shots.

The Grunter. Every throw from The Grunter is accompanied by a guttural vocalization, a manifestation of intensity and determination. This player, often clad in practical sportswear and rocking a no-nonsense haircut, exudes a conservative aura of discipline and individual responsibility. The Grunter's focus on personal effort and the audible exertion with each toss reflect a belief in meritocracy and the value of hard work.

The Squealer. Marked by high-pitched exclamations of excitement or dismay, The Squealer wears emotions on the sleeve. The Squealer's expressive nature, coupled with a penchant for trendy, socially conscious brands, suggests a liberal sensitivity to the communal aspects of the game. The Squealer's vocal reactions create a shared experience, emphasizing empathy and collective engagement over the solitary pursuit of victory.

The Gerrymanderer. Always tries to geographically position the boards so they get the benefit of terrain anomalies, gravity, the sun, or whatever else. Conservative.

The Leg Whipper. The Leg Whipper incorporates an elaborate leg movement into each throw, a peculiar flourish that seems to serve more style than function. This player, often sporting designer athleisure and a statement watch, might lean conservative, valuing the appearance of action and the embellishment of traditional forms. The Leg Whipper's performative technique underscores a preference for established practices, albeit with a personal twist.

The Mesothelioma Thwarter. Brings their own handmade beanbags in case the standard issue ones have asbestos in them. Liberal.

The Squatter. Adopting a low, crouching stance, The Squatter appears grounded and unshakeable. The Squatter's pragmatic, stretchy attire and sturdy footwear suggest a conservative bent, valuing stability, practicality, and reliability. The Squatter's methodical approach, emphasizing a solid foundation over flair, mirrors conservative principles of pragmatism and resilience.

The Jeff Gillooly.[7] Always places. But at what cost?

---

7   Jeff Gillooly, born in 1967, is a figure primarily known for his involvement in one of the most infamous scandals in the history of American sports. His role in the attack on figure skater Nancy

The Jeff Lebowski. This player epitomizes a laid-back, unorthodox approach to bowling er uh I mean cornhole. Their style is as relaxed and carefree as their persona, often bowling with a nonchalant flair that mirrors his overall life philosophy. The player's approach to the boards and the beanbags is devoid of the competitive intensity typically associated with the sport, favoring instead a casual, almost Zen-like engagement with the game. Their technique, while not technically polished, exudes a certain effortless charm, embodying the ethos of "taking it easy" and finding contentment in the simple pleasures of life. Liberal.

The Jeff Bezos. Has their own monogrammed cornhole beanbags and customized boards painted with a high gloss enamel with which the Stickler takes issue. Liberal.

The Jennifer Lopez. This player makes holes in the lawn with her Louboutins.

The Jennifer Beals. Insists on playing in the rain, and when it rains, the rain cascades down upon her in a dramatic torrent. The water, shimmering under the cornhole lights, envelops her in a sparkling veil, accentuating her every movement and adding a layer of raw intensity to her cornhole throws. Each throw of each beanbag reveals both vulnerability and unparalleled power and

---

Kerrigan in 1994 marked a significant moment in the annals of sporting controversies, intertwining crime with competitive athletics in a manner unprecedented in its media coverage and public fascination. Gillooly, at the time, was the ex-husband of figure skater Tonya Harding, an athlete who was Kerrigan's direct competitor on the ice. The attack was conceived as a means to incapacitate Kerrigan, thereby enhancing Harding's chances of success in the forthcoming 1994 Winter Olympics in Lillehammer. On January 6, 1994, Kerrigan was struck on the knee with a telescopic baton by assailant Shane Stant, leading to her withdrawal from the U.S. Figure Skating Championship–a critical event that served as a qualifier for the Olympics. The planning and execution of this assault implicated several individuals, with Gillooly being a central figure. Investigations revealed that he was intricately involved in the orchestration of the attack, collaborating closely with Harding's bodyguard, Shawn Eckardt, to hire Stant for the assault. The unraveling of these details in the media painted a sordid picture of the lengths to which individuals might go to secure competitive advantage, casting a long shadow over the integrity of competitive sports.In the aftermath of the attack, Gillooly was arrested and faced legal proceedings for his role in the conspiracy. He pleaded guilty to racketeering, receiving a sentence that reflected the gravity of his actions. His involvement in the attack not only led to significant legal consequences but also resulted in lasting infamy, overshadowing any other aspects of his personal or professional life. The incident, often referred to as "the whack heard around the world," remains a dark chapter in sports history, serving as a cautionary tale about the perils of unchecked ambition and the extreme measures some might resort to in the pursuit of victory. Gillooly's role in this scandal underscores the complex interplay between personal relationships, competitive pressures, and ethical boundaries in the high-stakes world of elite sports.

symbolizes the culmination of the cornhole player's struggles and aspirations. The rain captures her liberation and the pure joy of cornhole, emblematic of perseverance and the transcendent power of cornhole. Cornhole....What a Feeling!

The Jenna Bush Hager. This player, who has sort of almost grown on you after you reluctantly let them into the cornhole group because even you are not immune to nepotism, makes book recommendations while you're trying to focus on the game.

The Fist Pumper. Celebrating each successful toss with a vigorous fist pump, this player exudes confidence and competitiveness. The choice of bold, assertive apparel and accessories, perhaps a luxury sports watch or high-performance sneakers, hints at a conservative disposition, with a focus on achievement and a penchant for displays of strength and victory.

The Rudy Giuliani at a Press Conference. This is when you play cornhole at night and you set up lights in the backyard and the heat from the lights and the pressure of the game make the player's hair dye roll down their face and they lose credibility.

The Stickler. With an encyclopedic knowledge of the rules and a keen eye for infractions, The Stickler ensures the game adheres to the letter of the law. This player, often dressed in practical, no-frills attire, embodies conservative values of order and authority. The Stickler's insistence on regulation and fair play reflects a broader respect for structure and governance.

The Havarti. This player, despite several admonitions from cornhole league leaders and a box of wet wipes less-than-subtly placed within their reach, gets cheese, bean dip, spinach dip, condiments, and other foodstuff residue on the beanbags.

The Paul Westerberg. The life of the party, The Paul Westerberg, plays cornhole with a beverage in hand, embodying a carefree spirit. The Paul Westerberg's relaxed attire and disheveled look suggest a liberal embrace of leisure and spontaneity. The Paul Westerberg's jovial disregard for precision and rules champions a liberal preference for experience and enjoyment over competition and structure.

The Tranquil One. Approaching the game with a Zen-like calm, The Tranquil One remains unperturbed by victory or defeat. This player, often in comfortable, eco-friendly clothing, reflects a liberal mindfulness and a holistic view of life's pursuits. The Tranquil One's serene demeanor and non-competitive stance align with liberal ideals of harmony and balance.

The Energizer Twins. This is when you play cornhole with twins and they both wear tank tops and have blonde hair.

The Giggler. The Giggler finds amusement in every aspect of the game, much to the chagrin of the Stickler and the Fist Pumper. The Giggler's infectious laughter lightens the competitive atmosphere. Adorned in whimsical, eclectic attire, this player embodies a liberal joyfulness and a rejection of the seriousness that often characterizes competitive endeavors. The Giggler's playful approach to cornhole, prioritizing fun and camaraderie, champions the liberal values of inclusivity and community.

How to Tell if someone is Liberal or Conservative While Playing Pickleball

If a person purchases a non-basic paddle—like the kind with the nice carbon fiber—and babies throughout the first two matches (air-fiving with their teammate, touching handles at the end, wiping it down after each match) but then towards the endIof the third match, tries an aggressive slice and accidentally throws their paddle over the fence, is relieved to see that the paddle is okay, continues to play the third match, and at the end of the match, someone steps on the paddle while the person is helping disassemble the net, that person is conservative.

If during open play, your partner exhorts you to "hit it to the weaker player," and you continue to play as usual nonetheless, and your partner scoffs at you, your partner is conservative.

If someone grunts during pickleball, that person is Monica Seles. If that person is not Monica Seles, then that person is Carlos Alcarez. If that person is neither Monica Seles nor Carlos Alcarez, then that person is liberal.

Otherwise, Pickleball players can be categorized as follows:

The Poacher. The Poacher is known for their aggressive style, always ready to intercept the ball. They excel in doubles play, often crossing into their partner's territory to make a shot. This assertiveness on the court might suggest a conservative approach, valuing control and dominance in gameplay, mirroring a preference for traditional roles and structures.

The Waltzer. The Waltzer moves gracefully and easily across the court as if dancing to an inaudible rhythm. They play pickleball more like an art form than a competitive sport. Their liberal playing style, favoring creativity and fluidity over rigid tactics, might extend to a broader openness to change and diversity in thought and action.

The Jumper. Known for their athleticism, The Jumper can often be seen leaping off the ground to reach high balls. This high-energy player brings an element of unpredictability and excitement to the game. Their willingness to take risks and embrace the unknown on the court could reflect a liberal mindset, open to new ideas and experiences.

The Strategist. The Strategist approaches the game with meticulous planning. Every shot is calculated, and they excel in positioning and outthinking their opponents. This methodical approach to pickleball might align with conservative values, emphasizing strategy, order, and calculated risk over spontaneity.

The Powerhouse. The Powerhouse dominates the game with sheer force, driving the ball with unmatchable speed and strength. Their aggressive and direct style might suggest a conservative inclination, preferring to overpower challenges directly rather than navigate them with nuance or diplomacy.

The Trickster. The Trickster is all about deception, using a variety of spins and feints to confuse their opponents. They find joy in the unpredictability and creativity of their play. This penchant for innovation and surprise on the court might mirror a liberal perspective, valuing flexibility and adaptability.

The Anchor. Steady and reliable, The Anchor is the foundation of any doubles team. They may not make the flashiest plays, but their consistency and dependability make them invaluable. Their playing style, emphasizing stability and reliability, could be seen as conservative, upholding the importance of foundational principles and steady progress.

The Socialite. For The Socialite, pickleball is as much about the community and camaraderie as it is about the sport. They thrive on the social interaction and often play for the joy of being part of a team. Their emphasis on community and connection might align with liberal ideals, focusing on inclusivity and the collective well-being.

The Innovator. Always on the lookout for new techniques and strategies, The Innovator constantly evolves their game. They're not afraid to try unconventional shots or tactics, pushing the boundaries of traditional pickleball play. This constant quest for improvement and change could suggest a liberal mindset, eager for progress and innovation.

The Zen Master. The Zen Master plays with a calm demeanor, maintaining composure under pressure. They are the epitome of "playing your own game," focusing inwardly to control the pace and flow of the match. This introspective approach might align with conservative values, emphasizing self-reliance, discipline, and a measured response to external stimuli.

How to Tell Whether Someone is Liberal or Conservative While Skiing

If someone skis in jeans, they're conservative.

If they ski in jorts, they're liberal.

If someone skis in Patagonia, they're liberal.

If someone skis in Arc'teryx, they're conservative.

If someone skis in North Face, it's hard to tell. Ask how they feel about Vince Staples. If they say "I love him. Both his music and his comedy," they're liberal. If they say, "Who's that?" they're conservative.

If someone skis in Helley Henson, they're ski patrol. Always yield to them.

If a little kid calls you a "Jerry," he's of course too young to have political affiliations, but he will grow up to be either the president of his college's Young Republicans club or an ultra-liberal, eco-conscious #SkiLife #VanLife influencer.

If a woman at the après bar wearing a sweatshirt that says "APRES" is drinking a Hot Toddy, she's conservative. If she's drinking Irish Coffee, she's liberal.

If a couple at theaAprès bar wearing matching fur vests buys you a Bloody Mary from across the bar and invites you to their timeshare, politely say no. We cannot stress the polite part enough.

If you meet a girl on the chairlift and she offers you a shot of Fireball, say yes.

If you meet a guy on the chairlift and he offers you mushrooms, saying yes or no is up to you, but he's definitely liberal.

If you meet a guy on the chairlift and he offers you a bump of coke, saying yes or no is still up to you, but he's definitely conservative.

If you end up on the gondola with a group of college kids who call it "The Ganjala" before smoking multiple joints, they're all liberal.

If a man is skiing with a black leather bomber and steampunk goggles, he's the Bond villain you saw working out at the gym in a turtleneck, and he's coming for you.

If someone jokes about "the Blacks" being dangerous, they're conservative. Also, c'mon. Grow up.

If someone jokes that "They only ride the blues with their therapist" they're liberal. That one's pretty funny.

How to Tell if a Person is Liberal or Conservative While Playing Board Games

If a person's first guess while playing *Guess Who?* is "Does your person look like they might have an accent?" that person is conservative.

If a person's first guess while playing *Guess Who?* is "Does your person look healthy thanks in large measure to the Affordable Care Act?" that person is liberal.

If a person periodically exclaims, "You sunk my battleship!" whether that person is playing *Battleship* or not, that person is conservative.

If a person flips the *Monopoly* board over mid-game, rages out of the room, and doesn't talk to anyone until the next morning, that person is conservative.

If a person strikes a secret deal with a parent to bail them out of financial hardship in real life in exchange for not charging that parent any rent in all future family *Monopoly* games, that person is liberal.

If a person is genuinely and rightfully frightened of Lord Licorice while playing *Candyland*, that person is a conservative.

If a person thinks that *Candyland* is a metaphor for capitalism, that person is a liberal.

If a person thinks *Operation* is a dark metaphor for the American healthcare system, that person is a liberal.

If a person thinks *Operation* is a warning about the dangers of the Affordable Care Act, that person is a conservative.

If a person spells "covfefe" while playing *Scrabble*, they need to try again because that is not a word.

If a person thinks the guy lying on the *Operation* board was inspired by a nude Newt Gingrich, that person would be correct[8].

---

8   Newt, a man known for his extraordinary political prowess, sultry sex appeal, and clumsiness, became an unwitting muse for the iconic game Operation one fateful day while attempting to change a lightbulb standing on a wobbly stool in the Rayburn House Office Building. Newt managed to strain his

How to Tell if a Football Fan is Liberal or Conservative

If someone wears a giant foam cheese on their head, and the cheese is an exotic cheese, that person fancies themselves a Wisconsin liberal. They may not necessarily be from Wisconsin, but they fancy themselves a Wisconsin liberal.

If someone wears a giant foam cheese on their head, and the cheese is Velveeta, that person is conservative.

If someone wears a giant foam cheese on their head, and the cheese is adorned with Senator Joseph McCarthy election pins, that person is conservative.

If someone wears a giant foam cheese on their head and the Green Bay Packers are not playing in their vicinity, that person just really likes cheese.

If a person who looks like Aaron Rodgers does nothing but talk about Aaron Rodgers then that person might be Aaron Rodgers.

If someone can identify Miami Dolphins' Head Coach Mike McDaniels's Rose Gold Breitling Navitimer 1952 Quantieme Perpetual watch, that person is a liberal.

If someone thinks Taylor Swift dating Travis Kelce is part of a deep state plot involving Roger Goodell, George Soros, Joe Biden, and Brittany Mahomes, they are conservative.

If someone thinks Taylor Swift is dating Travis Kelce for his money, they are conservative.

If someone calls Brock Purdy "Mr. Irrelevant," that person is likely irrelevant.

Adam's apple while shouting for help, get a charley horse while lunging for balance, and somehow, in the commotion, bump his funny bone and get water on the knee. The attending ER doctor, bemused by the absurdity of Newt's predicament, sketched a humorous rendition of Newt on a napkin, riddled with comical ailments from "bread basket" to "spare ribs." A game developer, visiting a friend in the hospital, caught sight of the sketch. Inspired by Newt's oddly specific and hilarious set of misfortunes, he decided Newt was the perfect blueprint for a new game character. Thus, the Operation game's patient was born, immortalizing Newt's legendary clumsiness. Players around the world now tweeze out ailments with bated breath, none the wiser that each buzzer and laugh is a tribute to Newt's knack for finding himself in the most bizarre predicaments.

If someone says they have seen Macaulay Culkin and Joe Burrow together in the same room, they are lying because Macaulay Culkin and Joe Burrow are the same person.

If someone considers themselves pro-life but has not prayed for Damar Hamlin for at least 20 minutes every day for since Damar Hamlin died on that football field for a couple minutes, that person is not pro-life.

[Pause here to pray for Damar Hamlin]

If someone hates the Dallas Cowboys because of that AP photo from September 9, 1957 wherein a 14-year-old Jerry Jones is seen as part of a group of white students confronting Black students outside North Little Rock High School as those Black students try to integrate the school, well that's fine.

If someone hates the Dallas Cowboys for any other reason, well that's also fine.

If you haven't seen the video of the 1985 Chicago Bears, including William "The Refrigerator" Perry, Jim McMahon, Walter Payton, and Willie Gault, singing and shuffling to "The SuperBowl Shuffle," you really need to check it out on YouTube. It's fun.

If you haven't seen, or more pertinently heard, Whitney Houston sing "The Star Spangled Banner" at the 1991 SuperBowl, you really need to check it out on YouTube.

If a person has ever partied with Gronk, they are conservative.

If a person is from Buffalo, has ever attended a Bills game when the Bills were hosting the Patriots during the Brady era, and has thrown a dildo with "Brady" written on it onto the field, that person is liberal[9].

---

9   Conservatives, often characterized by traditional values and a preference for preserving established norms, tend to exhibit sexual repression. This phenomenon can be traced to several cultural, religious, and sociopolitical influences that shape conservative ideologies. Many conservatives adhere to strict moral codes derived from religious teachings, which often emphasize chastity, modesty, and traditional gender roles. These values promote a conservative approach to sexuality, viewing it primarily within the confines of marriage and often stigmatizing premarital sex, homosexuality, and non-traditional sexual expressions, like dildo tossing.

The social environment within conservative communities also plays a significant role. In these settings, there is often a strong emphasis on maintaining public decency and upholding family values, which can lead to the suppression of open discussions about sex and sexuality. This cultural backdrop discourages

If a person ever gets Kirk Cousins and Kirk Cameron confused, that is ok because they are both egomaniacs who have yet to realize they are fucking worthless.

If a person sings along to Carrie Underwood's "Waiting All Day for Sunday Night" *Sunday Night Football* theme on NBC, that person is liberal.

If you are a woman, Harrison Butker demands that you put this book down and get back in the kitchen.

If someone said they would never wear Nike sneakers ever again, after Nike featured Colin Kaepernick in advertising shortly after Colin Kepernick kneeled for the National Anthem and encouraged others to do so during the 2016 season, that person is conservative.

If you have wondered whether those someones have worn NIke sneakers since saying they never would, after Nike featured Colin Kaepernick in its advertising in 2016 and are nearly certain that most of them have, you are likely liberal.

If you touch a pigskin on the sabbath you are going to hell. Leviticus 11:7-8.

---

individuals from exploring or expressing their sexual desires openly, fostering an environment where sexual repression is prevalent.

Political factors further reinforce this repression. Conservative policies frequently oppose comprehensive sex education, access to contraceptives, and LGBTQ+ rights, framing such measures as threats to societal morality. By limiting exposure to diverse perspectives on sexuality, these policies perpetuate a narrow, restrictive view of sexual behavior.

The result is a complex interplay of religious, cultural, and political factors that contribute to sexual repression among conservatives. This repression not only affects personal sexual health and well-being but also influences broader societal attitudes towards sexuality, shaping public discourse and policy in ways that reinforce conservative sexual norms.

How To Tell if Someone is Liberal or Conservative at a Collegiate a Cappella Competition

If a person is cheering for Liberty University's premiere a cappella group Shine, that person is conservative.

If a person is cheering for any of Oberlin College's a cappella groups, to whit, The Obertones, Pitch Please, 'Round Midnight, The Acapelicans, and Nothing but Treble, that person is liberal.

If someone has a favorite Tufts Beelzebub, that person is liberal.

If someone's main complaint about the Dartmouth Sings' rendition of Fountains of Wayne's "Stacy's Mom" is that the song is sexist and objectifying to women while also normalizing a predatory relationship between an adult woman and a young boy, that person is a liberal.

If someone's main complaint about Dartmouth Sings' rendition of Fountain of Wayne's "Stacy's Mom" is that Josh sounds a little too good, that person is conservative.

If an alumnus from the University of Chicago's Voices in Your Head who sang with the group the year they sang Ben Folds's "Magic" returns to the competitive collegiate a cappella scene as a judge, that person will judge liberally.

If an alumnus from the University of Virginia's New Dominions who sang with the group the year they sang Mika's "Happy Endings" returns to the competitive collegiate a cappella scene as a judge, that person will judge conservatively.

If a current member of the University of Rochester's Midnight Ramblers wonders if the group will ever reach the same heights as they did in 2008 when the Ramblers' rendition of Panic! At the Disco's "I Write Sins Not Tragedies" was selected as one of the Best of Collegiate a Cappella songs of the year, that current member is a liberal while ¾ of all the members of that 2008 squad still call themselves liberal though all have become way more conservative than they ever thought possible.

If a person has boycotted collegiate a cappella competitions since 1998 because they believe that Smith college's Smiffenpoofs were robbed when their rendition of Pat Benatar's "Love is a Battlefield" lost to the University of Pennsylvania's Counterparts's rendition of Joan Osborne's "One of Us" in the International Championship of Collegiate A Cappella (ICCA) that year, that person is liberal but has likely married a conservative.

If someone is wondering why no collegiate a cappella band has ever one a mash-up of the Indigo Girls's "Galileo" with Coldplay's "The Scientist," well, that makes two of us[10].

---

10   Maybe we should ask Justin who put the kabosh on the idea. Never mind the fact that by mashing up the two we could have created an a cappella arrangement so compelling we would have returned home from ICCA as champions. The two songs, while distinct in their musical styles and themes, share an emotional depth and lyrical introspection that could blend harmoniously, offering a rich tapestry of sound and meaning. But no, Justin. Let's sing another Ben Folds tune.

"Galileo," with its folk-rock essence, delves into themes of introspection, questioning, and the search for understanding, both in a scientific and personal sense. Its melodic lines are poignant and carry a sense of yearning that could beautifully complement the more modern, alternative rock vibe of "The Scientist." The latter is a raw, emotive ballad that speaks to the desire to go back in time and fix what went wrong, echoing the human longing for redemption and understanding. But hey. When in Rome we do as Justin does, don't we?

The juxtaposition of these themes - the quest for scientific understanding and personal redemption - would have provided a powerful narrative backbone for the mash-up. Just spit-balling here, but the arrangement likely would have start with the haunting piano intro of "The Scientist," immediately setting a reflective tone, before we weaved in the iconic guitar riff of "Galileo." This would have not only showcased the group's versatility in blending different musical styles but also highlighted our ability to reinterpret these elements in a purely vocal form. On the other hand, several people said our new spin on Ben Folds's "Still Fightin' It" was really cool too. My mom said it was neat.

Harmonically, both songs offer rich opportunities for complex vocal arrangements. "The Scientist," with its minimalist instrumentation, relies heavily on its poignant melody and chord progressions, which could have been beautifully expressed through vocal harmonies. "Galileo," on the other hand, provides a more rhythmic and harmonic complexity that can add depth and contrast to the arrangement. By alternating between the driving rhythms of "Galileo" and the sweeping melodies of "The Scientist," we would have gathered so much momentum and kept the audience on thedge of their seats. Additionally, Justin's idea for the baritones to sing "yum yum yum yum yum yum" during the line where Ben Folds sings "The roast beef combo's only $9.95" was fucking genius. No one has ever done that before.

The emotional climax of the mash-up would have come from combining the choruses of both songs, overlaying "Nobody said it was easy" with "I'm not making a joke, you know me, I take everything so seriously." This would create a moment of intense emotional resonance, highlighting the universal struggles of understanding and the human condition.

But hey, when all the baritones sang that line where Ben Folds says "Everybody knows it sucks to grow up." really resonated, Justin.

Furthermore, the arrangement could have incorporated dynamic shifts, from the soft, introspective verses to the powerful, harmonized choruses, showcasing our vocal range and emotional expressivity.

If a person hears the Loyola Chimes's senior members' mash-up of REO Speedwagon's "Can't Fight this Feeling" and Ceine Dion's "It's All Coming Back to Me Now" and doesn't get a little misty-eyed then that person is surely emotionally unavailable and likely has difficulty sustaining meaningful bonds in relationships.

This dynamic journey could have captivated the audience and demonstrated our group's mastery of vocal technique as well as our ability to convey deep emotion. And by "deep emotion" I mean "whatever the fuck Justin wants."

In the competitive arena of collegiate a cappella, where innovation and emotional impact are key, this mash-up could stand out for its creativity, technical proficiency, and the heartfelt message it conveys. By blending "Galileo" and "The Scientist," we could have offered a unique, memorable performance that resonated with the judges and audience alike, making it a strong contender for the championship title. Also, Justin sucks.

How to Tell if Someone is Liberal or Conservative While Hanging Out With Levi Johnston (Regardless of political affiliations, you fuck with Levi Johnston and he'll kick your ass.)

If a group of you is hanging out with Levi Johnston, and Levi Johnston asks, "hey what you fellas feel like doing today?" and the person says, "I just want to hang out with the boys," that person is a liberal.

If a group of you is hanging out with Levi Johnston, and Levi Johnston asks, "hey what you fellas feel like doing today?" and the person says, "I want to play some hockey," that person is a liberal.

If a group of you is hanging out with Levi Johnston, and Levi Johnston asks, "hey what you fellas feel like doing today?" and the person says, "I want to do some fishing," that person is a conservative.

If a group of you is hanging out with Levi Johnston, and Levi Johnston asks, "hey what you fellas feel like doing today?" and the person says, "I just want to kill some moose," that person is a conservative.

If a group of you is hanging out with Levi Johnston, and Levi Johnston asks, "hey what you fellas feel like doing today?" and the person says, "Let's just shoot the shit," that person is a liberal.

If a group of you is hanging out with Levi Johnston, and Levi Johnston asks, "hey what you fellas feel like doing today?" and the person says, "I just want to do some chillin', I guess," that person is a conservative.

Mr. Jones

Counting Crows's "Mr. Jones" kicks off with a yearning for the bohemian life, "Down at the New Amsterdam, staring at this yellow-haired girl," which sets the stage for Mr. Jones' liberal leanings. The desire to "be a big star" and the fascination with the flamboyant, the artistic, and the unconventional speaks to a liberal's embrace of diverse expressions of identity and success. Mr. Jones's conversations, filled with dreams of fame and understanding, mirror the liberal pursuit of self-actualization and a deep-seated belief in the importance of personal growth and freedom. The lyric, "When everybody loves me, I will never be lonely," underscores a universal longing for acceptance and connection, aligning with liberal values that champion inclusivity and community.

Furthermore, the song's reflection on existential themes and the search for meaning beyond the material, illustrated by the line, "We all wanna be big stars, but we don't know why and we don't know how," resonates with the liberal inclination towards introspection and questioning the status quo.

Gloria #1

Laura Branigan's "Gloria" is an energetic anthem that pulsates with the story of a woman who's both enigmatic and wildly spirited. Through the vibrant lyrics and the compelling narrative of the song, one could playfully surmise that Gloria embodies the heart and soul of liberalism.

The song portrays Gloria as someone living on the edge, dancing through life with a rebellious streak, as captured in the lines, "Gloria, you're always on the run now. Running after somebody, you gotta get him somehow." This relentless pursuit of what she desires, defying conventions and societal expectations, mirrors the liberal ethos of personal freedom and the courage to chase one's dreams, no matter the odds.

Gloria's story, filled with whispers and rumors of her escapades, to wit, "Will you meet him on the main line, or will you catch him on the rebound? Will you marry for the money, take a lover in the afternoon?" reflects the sexual liberation of which liberals are so proud. It's a celebration of individuality and the strength to carve one's own path in life.

Moreover, the song's upbeat tempo and Branigan's powerful delivery imbue Gloria with an infectious energy that champions the liberal values of empowerment, resilience, and the unwavering spirit to live life on one's own terms. In essence, Gloria, through the dynamic narrative of Branigan's hit song, becomes an archetype of liberalism—a beacon of self-expression, boldness, and the indefatigable pursuit of personal liberty in the face of life's many challenges.

Gloria #2

The Gloria in the Doors's "Gloria," a raw and impassioned rock classic, is mysterious, captivating, and brimming with an untamed spirit. Through the gritty lens of this song, it's clear that Gloria embodies a fiercely independent streak that aligns with libertarian principles.

The song's repetitive and insistent chorus, "G-L-O-R-I-A, Gloria!" resonates with a sense of individualism and personal freedom, core tenets of libertarianism. Gloria's allure, underscored by the song's raw energy and unbridled passion, suggests a persona that defies conventional norms and lives by her own rules, much like the libertarian ideal of minimal constraints and maximal personal autonomy.

The line "She comes around here, just about midnight" paints Gloria as a night owl, a free spirit who thrives in the shadowy margins of society's timetable, further emphasizing her autonomy and the libertarian value of self-determination outside societal expectations.

Moreover, the song's unpolished, garage-band aesthetic, combined with its straightforward, almost defiant declaration of Gloria's name, mirrors the libertarian emphasis on authenticity, personal identity, and resistance to overbearing authority or cultural homogenization. In sum, "Gloria" as presented by The Doors, through its visceral sound and portrayal of a woman who commands attention and lives fiercely on her own terms, subtly champions the libertarian virtues of independence, personal freedom, and the intrinsic value of the individual.

Part Four -

CELEBRATIONS AND HOLIDAYS

How to Tell Whether Someone is a Liberal or Conservative on Halloween

If someone has fall-themed hand towels in their bathroom, they are a liberal.

If someone wears a spooky vampire costume, they are conservative.

If someone listens to Vampire Weekend they are liberal.

If a man has a favorite pair of overalls, he is a conservative. If a man wears a pair of overalls in conjunction with one of those inflatable horse rider costumes, the man is a liberal.

If a man wears his favorite leather jacket to dress up as the Fonz for at least five straight years, that man is a liberal.

If a woman dresses up like Catwoman, she is conservative.

If a man dresses up as shirtless Joe Biden for Halloween, he is liberal.

If a man dresses up like a football player, he is conservative. UNLESS: the football player plays for a team whose mascot is from the feline family then that man is liberal.

If a person dresses up like the the Creature from The Black Lagoon they are liberal.

If a person dresses up like Evel Knievel, that person is conservative.

If a woman watches all seven seasons of *Gilmore Girls* between October 1 and October 31, she is conservative. If a man does the same, he is liberal.

If anyone shed a tear during *Gilmore Girls'* Season 4, Episode 22, the episode called "Raincoats and Recipes," well, that makes them human. (They won't be dressing up or going out this Halloween, and that's *OK.*)

If anyone cheers for the Kansas City Chiefs because they enjoy watching a revolutionary offense led by generational talent Patrick Mahomes, they are conservative. If anyone dresses up as Travis Kelce, they are liberal. If they dress up as Travis Kelce and their life partner recess up as Taylor Swift, they are still liberal. If they dress up as Travis Kelce and their business partner dresses up as Jason Kelce, they are both conservative. Unless the business in which the Travis Kelce costume guy and the Jason Kelce costume guy involves operations management consulting, risk and compliance consulting, or data analytics consulting, then both are liberal.

If anyone dresses up as legendary coach Kansas City Chiefs coach Andy Reid, they are conservative. Unless they integrate a rack of spare ribs slathered with Kansas City BBQ sauce into the costume, then they are liberal.

If anyone dresses up as Dorothy from *Wizard of Oz* they are liberal. However, if someone dresses up as Dorothy and refers to her as "the original Kansas Hottie" all evening and places great emphasis on the blue and white gingham halter top and Ruby stilettos, that person is a conservative.

If someone's fridge contains over six (6) pumpkin spice beers, they are conservative. Unless they brewed the beers themselves, then they are liberal.

If someone dresses up like the bad guy from the SAW horror film franchise, they are anarcho-communist.

If someone has a personal best corn maze escape time, they are conservative.

If someone dresses up as Nicole Kidman in the AMC Movie Theater Ad they are liberal.

If a person makes a costume themselves and integrates a couple hundred square feet of cardboard, a complex system of levers and pulleys, hydraulics, and a baby stroller or wagon intot the costume, they are liberal.

If someone's favorite Halloween movie is *Halloween*, they are conservative. If they dress up like Michael Myers every year, they are extra-super-conservative.

If someone's favorite Halloween movie is It's *The Great Pumpkin, Charlie Brown* they are somehow both liberal and conservative. What tips the scales if what they wear on Halloween. If they wear a sheet ghost costume, they are liberal. If they dress up as a witch, they are conservative. Unless either one has a Snoopy tattoo, in which case they are conservative, Unless, they have a Snoopy tattoo AND a Woodstock tattoo, in which case they are liberal an staunch advocates of the left wing laissez-faire school of thought as identified in Adam Smith's seminal 1776 work, *The Wealth of Nations.*

If someone eats candy corn by the handful and appears to enjoy it, they are liberal.

If someone dresses up as Uma Thurman as *Pulp Fiction's* Mia Wallace, that person is conservative. Unless they include the syringe coming out of the sternum, in which case they are liberal.

If someone brings a charcuterie board to a Halloween party and uses prosciutto and cheese to replicate witches fingers, they are liberal.

If someone dresses up as a Dallas Cowboy Cheerleader, they are conservative.

If someone drinks Miller Lite because it tastes great and dresses up as Elvira, Mistress of the Dark, they are liberal. If someone dresses up as Elvira. Mistress of the Dark and drinks Miller Lite but drinks Miller Lite because it is less filling, that person is a conservative. If someone drinks Miller Lite because they like a good beer buzz early in the mornin', that person is Sheryl Crow whose political leanings remain nebulous. She seems liberal but remains coy when asked if she dated Kid Rock in or around 2002, when they collaborated on "Picture."

If someone buys Halloween candy in September but eats it all by October 1, they are a liberal.

If someone hears Sade's "Smooth Operator" during an Uber ride on the way to a costume party, that person is a liberal. Unless they are dressed as Pennywise the Clown, in which that person is a conservative.

If someone leaves their sunroof open on Halloween night and some neighborhood hooligans fill their car with leaves, that person is a conservative.

If someone FaceTimes you without warning, uninvite them from your Halloween party.

How to Tell if Someone is Liberal or Conservative On Thanksgiving

If someone prefers their cranberry sauce in the shape of a can, they are conservative.

If a man wears L.L. Bean's signature Bean Boots, they're liberal until Election Day.

If a man wears authentic military boots from the army surplus store, they're conservative until "shit goes down." Then it won't matter which side you're on, son.

If someone shows up to Thanksgiving dinner wearing a flannel shirt from Aime Leon Dore, they are liberal.

If someone thinks that flannel costs $40 and not $400, they are conservative.

If a man "knows a nice brewery nearby we can all go to instead," he is liberal.

If someone brings a pot of atomic chili to Thanksgiving dinner, they are conservative. And awesome.

If someone wistfully remembers that time Betty White and Lorne Green hosted the Macy's Thanksgiving Day parade, they are conservative.

If someone brings some squash from their home garden, they are liberal.

If someone brings enough squash to feed five families from their home garden, they are conservative.

If every year someone says "pass the dinner rolls" and your dad chucks a solitary dinner roll at them, then your dad is conservative and the person who says "pass the dinner rolls" is liberal.

If someone wistfully wonders what a Macy's Thanksgiving Day balloon of Ruth Bader Ginsburg might look like and can almost see it floating down Broadway while dozens of RBGs hold the balloon strings and march it down Broadway while Britney Spears sings a holiday-tinged version of her hit song "Gimme More," they are liberal.

If someone pronounces the pecan in pecan pie like "pe-KANN" they are conservative.

If someone pronounces the pecan in pecan pie like "pe-CAWN" they are liberal.

If someone cheers for the Dallas Cowboys they are conservative. Obviously. Unless they cheer for the Dallas Cowboys because Dak Prescott has been very vocal about his struggles with mental illness, then they are liberal.

If someone cheers for the Detroit Lions they are liberal. Obviously. Unless they are cheering from prison because they were convicted of plotting to kidnap Michigan Governor Gretchen Whitmer. Then they are conservative.

If a man hasn't missed a Turkey Trot in 15 years, he is liberal. However, if a woman does the same, she is conservative.

If your uncle brings a strange man "From the Knights of Columbus" who hasn't blinked since arriving three hours ago, he is conservative.

If the strange man helps your mom clean the dishes while your uncle shows you a picture of your bald dad with a mullet and mustache, he is liberal.

If a man undoes his pants after eating Thanksgiving dinner, he is conservative.

If someone shoots the TV because of how their team is playing, they are conservative.

If your grandma threatens to shit in the turkey unless you let her watch *Jeopardy!*, then just let her watch Jeopardy!

If your uncle gets drunk on homemade Limoncillo, takes off his shirt, and starts singing snippets of Right Said Fred's "I'm Too Sexy," he is liberal.

If your uncle gets drunk on homemade Limoncillo, takes off his shirt, and starts singing snippets of "Milkshake" by Kelis, he is conservative.

If the woman your cousin just married takes a little airplane bottle of Crown Royal out of her purse and pours it on her turkey, then she is conservative.

If the woman your cousin just married takes a little airplane bottle of Crown Royal out of her purse and pours it on her mashed potatoes, then she is conservative.

If the woman your cousin just married takes a little airplane bottle of Wild Turkey out of her purse and pours it on her turkey, then she is an anarchist.

If that same woman your cousin just married steals a Costco-sized box of individually wrapped Cheez-Its from your garage as she and your cousin are leaving, then she is still conservative, but more of a moderate conservative, like former Maryland governor Larry Hogan.

If your grandpa says he's going to check your newborn son's diaper, takes your son to the other room, puts pumpkin pie filling in an empty diaper, walks back into the kitchen to report on the status of your newborn son's diaper, and then pretends to eat the pumpkin pie filling, he is liberal.

If anyone in the kitchen mimics *The Bear by saying* "Yes chef" as your family prepares Thanksgiving dinner, they are conservative.

If anyone in the kitchen mimics *The Bear* by serving Italian beef sandwiches in lieu of turkey, mashed potatoes, and green bean casserole, they are liberal.

If anyone in the kitchen or anywhere mimics *The Bear* by displaying pervasive self-doubt, crippling anxiety, and toxic coping mechanisms, then you know you are in the right place.

How to Tell if Someone is Liberal or Conservative On Christmas

If someone says their favorite Christmas movie is It's a *Wonderful Life*, they're conservative.

If someone says their favorite Christmas movie is *A Charlie Brown Christmas*, they're liberal.

If someone says their favorite Christmas movie is *The Polar Express*, something is wrong with them.

If someone mentions that last holiday season marked the 20th anniversary of Kid Rock's seminal Christmas carol, "Frosty the Blowman," they are conservative.

If someone mentions that this holiday season marks the 40th anniversary of Wham!'s seminal Christmas carol, "Last Christmas," they are liberal.

If a man wears a denim jacket to Christmas dinner, he's liberal. If he wears a tweed jacket, he's conservative. The opposite was the case for generations, but officially flipped around 2016.

If someone builds a snowman with a penis, they're liberal. If they build a snowman with boobs, they're conservative. This has always been the case.

If a woman drinks too much hard cider at Christmas dinner, she is liberal. If she drinks too much eggnog, she's conservative. If she drinks too much Rumplemintz, she's had a long year and it has nothing to do with politics.

If the family tree is a six-foot balsam, the parents are moderate and so are their kids.

If the family tree is a seven-foot Douglas fir, the parents are conservative but the kids are liberal.

If the family tree is an eight-foot Fraser fir, the parents are conservative and so are the kids.

If the family tree is artificial and therefore reusable, the parents are liberal but the kids will be conservative.

If your uncle always brings bourbon to Christmas dinner, he's conservative.

If your uncle always brings a variety pack of craft beers to Christmas dinner, he's liberal.

If your uncle always brings the same story about how your dad peed his pants on Santa's lap when they were kids, he needs new material.

If your neighborhood only hangs white lights over their homes, your neighbors would take up arms against the government if taxes were raised even 5%.

If your neighborhood hangs colorful lights and inflatable Santas, your neighbors are liberal and don't mind paying 5% more on their electric bills.

If your neighborhood has cars with big bows on them, you live on the set of a Lexus commercial.

If your neighborhood has cars with reindeer antlers hanging out the windows, you're liberal but unwilling to fight over politics.

If your neighborhood has cars with "I survived the war on Christmas." bumper stickers, you're liberal and more than willing to fight over politics.

If your neighborhood has one disturbingly powerful man who lives in a large house overlooking the factory he owns and the workers he barely pays, you either live along the rust belt of Pennsylvania or the North Pole of Earth.

Come to think of it, if you are Santa Claus himself, you're conservative. Pay your elves! Actually, you give away presents to the entire world for free. That's pretty liberal. You also judge who does and doesn't deserve gifts, which is borderline dictatorial. This is a tricky one. We suggest you discuss it with your relatives, but only after everyone's had at least two drinks.

A Constitutional Christmas

The Constitution is the sacred document that gives us Christmas. Here's why it is so very special.

Christmas Symbol	Constitutional Connection
Angel	Angels remind us of the First Amendment's protection of free speech for without it, they never could have sung over Bethlehem. The Constitution ensures that every heavenly message and earthly opinion can be shared without fear. This celestial symbolism underscores the importance of communication in democracy.
Baby Jesus	Just as Baby Jesus represents salvation, the Constitution upholds the sanctity of justice and liberty, akin to the due process promised in the 14th Amendment. He embodies the hope for fairness and redemption in the legal system.
Star of Bethlehem	The star is like the guiding light of the Constitution, illuminating the path to unalienable rights and the pursuit of happiness, as declared in the preamble. It's a celestial beacon for the foundational principles of America.
Three Kings	The three kings (especially the two Caucasian ones) worked hard to travel to visit Jesus. This journey reflects the Constitution's Article I, promoting commerce and interaction among states, ensuring that all who seek wisdom are free to travel and trade. It symbolizes the unity and economic interdependence of the states.
Shepherd	Shepherds symbolize the vigilant protection offered by the 2nd Amendment, guarding the flock with the same resolve that citizens defend their homes and liberties. This pastoral image highlights the right to personal and communal safety.
Nativity Scene	This scene is a tableau of the Constitution's framing, where diverse figures come together, echoing the Constitutional Convention's assembly for a common purpose. It represents the collaborative spirit of creating a unified nation.
Advent Wreath	The wreath's circular shape symbolizes the cylindrical shape of the barrel of an AK-47. It's the world's most popular assault rifle, a weapon all fighters love. An elegantly simple nine pound amalgamation of forged steel and plywood, it doesn't break, jam, or overheat. It will shoot whether it's covered in mud or filled with sand. It's so easy even a child can use it, and they do. While the barrel of an AK-47 is 16.34 inches long, wreaths can be any size because anyone can get shot, and they do.

Christmas Symbol	Constitutional Connection
Christmas Star	The star's high vantage symbolizes the Supreme Court's oversight, ensuring that Constitutional principles like free speech shine brightly over the land. It's a reminder of the judiciary's role in upholding fundamental rights.
Candy Cane	Its stripes remind us of the 13 original colonies, and its shape like a 'J' for justice, symbolizing the judiciary's role in upholding the Constitution. The candy cane combines sweet tradition with the solemn duty of legal protection.
Christmas Tree	Like the unwavering tree, the Constitution stands resilient, its branches of government spreading to uphold democracy and liberty under law. The evergreen nature of the tree reflects the lasting power of the Constitution's principles.
Manger	The humble manger reflects the foundational principle that all are equal under the Constitution, deserving of protection and dignity, because Mary & Joseph were refugees seeking shelter for their baby and how the Constitution says we have to keep out immigrants.
Gifts	The exchange of gifts from billionaire to Supreme Court justice symbolizes the reciprocal respect for rights among citizens. Gifts represent the Constitutional promise that all may freely exercise their rights, whether in speech, faith, or assembly, without government interference.
Bells	Bells ring out warnings and celebrations alike, echoing the First Amendment's guarantee of free speech, allowing all voices to be heard. The sound of bells is a call to protect and cherish the liberty and freedoms we hold dear.
Poinsettia	Its bright red color recalls the color of the jackets the British wore during the Revolutionary War when we fought to escape Britain because we didn't like the king telling us what religion to be. It is also why Joel Osteen drives a bright red Ferrari.
Dove	Doves remind us of the peaceful assembly and petitions for redress guaranteed by the First Amendment, ensuring that peace guides our constitutional discourse. They symbolize the gentle power of democracy in action. Also doves are what God uses when he touches the hand of the electorate - which just so happens to be whenever a Republican wins.

Christmas Symbol	Constitutional Connection
Frankincense	Frankincense's aroma ascending is like the aspirations of the Constitution, reaching toward a more perfect union where religious and civil liberties coexist harmoniously. It's an aromatic symbol of the sacredness of these aspirations. Also, don't like frankincense? Try Ivanka Trump Eau de Parfum Spray For Women, Just $179.99 for 3.4 Fluid Ounces on Amazon.
Myrrh	Myrrh, used in burial, reminds us of the sacrifices made to protect our Constitutional freedoms, particularly those of the Fourth Amendment, guarding against unreasonable searches. Its somber scent is a tribute to those who defend rights.
Gold	Gold represents the wealth of opportunities the Constitution's commerce clause protects, ensuring that trade and prosperity flow freely. It's a symbol of the economic freedoms and entrepreneurial spirit fostered by the Constitution.
Holly	Holly's sharp leaves remind us of the vigilant defense required to protect the liberties outlined in our founding document, especially in matters of free expression. The red berries symbolize the vitality and resilience of these rights.
Gingerbread Men	This reminds us that men write the Constitution, men like Gouveneur Morris who died in 1816 when he attempted to stick a piece of whale bone into his dick to dislodge a urinary tract blockage. Also God made Adam and then Eve and Eve sinned. Frosted gingerbread men remind us that men like Brett Kavanaugh get to act like total fucking douchebags while also simultaneously taking the moral highground on fucking everything, as God intended.
Yule Log	Like the enduring Yule log, the Constitution burns as a beacon of hope and guiding light, preserving the flames of freedom through the checks and balances system. It represents the warmth and enduring nature of American democracy.
Eggnog	Brett Kavanaugh just stuck his dick in the eggnog and said, "Did someone say cinnamon stick?" and it was so funny so that is the drink of Christmas.
Christmas Lights	These lights reflect the Constitution's role in enlightening society, ensuring that the path of justice is illuminated for all citizens. They are a twinkling testament to the bright and guiding principles of the Constitution.
Lamb	The lamb's innocence and sacrifice mirror the principles of due process and fairness central to the Constitution, protecting even the meekest among us. It's a gentle reminder of the nurturing care the legal system aims to provide.

Christmas Symbol	Constitutional Connection
Wreath	The wreath, with no beginning or end, symbolizes the enduring nature of our Constitutional rights, forever safeguarded and continuous. It represents the unbroken promise of liberty and justice for all Americans.
Tinsel	Tinsel's shimmer is like the gleaming promise of justice and liberty, ensuring that every American's rights are pure and untarnished under the law. The sparkle of tinsel is like the sparkling clarity of our constitutional protections.
Shepherd's Staff	The staff guides the flock as the Constitution guides the nation, ensuring every citizen is led to the fair pastures of justice and liberty. It represents the leadership and direction provided by the Constitution in our daily lives.

How to Tell if Someone is Liberal or Conservative on St. Patrick's Day

If the director of food services at one of the lower-tier ivies or an ivy adjacent university dyes the mashed potatoes green on St. Patrick's Day, and a student eats those mashed potatoes, that student is a blithering barnacle on a banshee's backside and and if they don't pray for forgiveness at the foot of the cross, then you better believe Beelzebub's got a bunk bed waiting for them!

If the director of food services at your college dyes the mashed potatoes green on St. Patrick's Day, and a student wants to eat the mashed potatoes, pokes, roots around in, and generally disturbs those mashed potatoes with their fork, and takes one bite, that student is a bumbling bagpipe buster and if they don't pledge their heart to the saints, then they'll soon be sharing a pint with Lucifer in his eternal pub of damnation!

If the director of food services at your college dyes the mashed potatoes green on St. Patrick's Day, and a student refuses those green mashed potatoes when the cafeteria worker offers to put a dollop on their plate, that student is a slithering slug on a shamrock shake who - if they don't start fingerin' their rosary beads and praying for forgiveness - will soon be dancing a jig straight to the devil's doorstep!!

If the director of food services at your college dyes the mashed potatoes green on St. Patrick's Day, and a student begins a student protest about food waste, that student is a blathering brogue with a broken buckle who - if they don't start seeking the blessings of our Holy Mother in Heaven - will be tailoring Satan's tartans in hell's haberdashery come judgment day!

If the director of food services at your work cafeteria dyes the mashed potatoes green on St. Patrick's Day, and one of your colleagues is passed out and doesn't make it to the cafeteria at all that day, that colleague is in perfect equipoise between liberal and conservative on the political philosophy continuum.

If it's St. Patty's day 1984 and a person has been living in NYC for a few months before going back to college in Chicago and that person is waiting at Grand Central for a train and becomes aware they are surrounded by several huge drunk NYPD firefighters who find their outfit (a bowler hat with wings (a youthful affectation), a kelly-green parka, green pants, and gold shoes) "LOOK!! A LEPRECHAUN!" and the firefighters' merriment evolves into some good-natured rough-handling and the many rounds of drinks until the person misses their train and has to sleep in Grand Central Station, that person is a liberal until about eight or nine years ago. The firefighters are, of course, all conservative. Especially the ones from Staten Island.

If a proud Irish person eschews traditional St. Patrick's Day revelry because they kind of hate St. Patrick's Day and people celebrating proud and noble Irish culture by getting stinking drunk until they're puking their guts out and in lieu thereof, dresses up like and pretends to be a banshee, a female ghost or fairy of Celtic folklore that wails and screams and is generally an omen of doom, horror, sorrow and other fun things, and source of the old phrase "scream like a banshee," because banshees are much more relatable than some incredibly stereotypical leprechaun, that person is a dizzy daffodil in a drizzle of dung who will soon be scrubbing the cauldrons of Mephistopheles's kitchen if they don't start washin' the feet of the weary in atonement for all their transgressions!

If a person was five years old when their dad got drunk and lost them in a crowd of St. Patrick's Day parade revelers and that person asks several strangers, a group of Irish dancers, and a police officer for help in finding their dad but ends up never seeing their dad again, that person is now in a U2 cover band.

If your name is Seamus and you are in a band called "The Tipsy Tinkerers" that only plays at a bar called O'Malley's on St. Patrick's Day, you are a tottering turnip in a tangle of tartan and you are going to hell!

If your name is Seamus and you are in a band called "Finnegan's Fiddlesticks" that only plays at a bar called O'Malley's on St. Patrick's Day, you are a rambling rabbit in a ruckus of rhubarb who is also going to hell!

If you have ever heard your Irish Setter talk to you on St. Patrick's Day, you are a loopy leprechaun with a lopsided leer ad if you don't shape up you'll be planting potatoes in the devil's garden unless you start reciting your morning devotions with a bit more fervor!

If your Irish Setter is named "Seamus" you are a whiskey-wrecked wretch, and you'll be the piper, piping away in perdition!

If your Irish Setter can play "Whiskey in a Jar" on the harp, you are a twittering twit in tweed trousers!

If you are a shy accountant by day but once a year - on St. Patrick's Day - you belt out a version of "Danny Boy" in a voice that rivals Pavarotti's in the Irish bar called the Blarney Stone where everyone from your company where you do your accounting is dancing, you are half-witted hedgehog in a hooligan's hat who's soon to be muckin' about in the underworld's peat bog unless you start chanting the Psalms with a purer heart!

If a person gets punched in the face stumbling out of an Irish bar on 103rd Street on St. Patrick's Day evening, that person is a mucky mandrake in a minstrel's mitten! The puncher, incidentally, is also a mucky mandrake in a minstrel's mitten. Both are bound for the brimstone bridge to Hades.

If a person runs into a Panera on a St. Patrick's Day parade route about mid-way through the St. Patrick's Day parade, bypasses the bathroom lines, walks intot he bathroom, hops on the sink to take a shit in the sink, and the sink falls off the wall so the person just shits on the floor as water and porcelain shards fly about, and walks out of Panera as though nothing happened, that person is a liberal.

If a person says, "Everyone's Irish on St. Patrick's Day!" while explaining the difference between ethnicity and citizenship, that person is conservative.

If a person says, "Everyone's Irish on St. Patrick's Day!" before they play "Zombie" by the Cranberries on the jukebox, that person is liberal.

If a person wakes up at 6:00 a.m. on St. Patrick's Day and starts drinking Guinness right away, that person is conservative. Unless that person goes to their friend's apartment around 8:00 a.m. and does back to back Irish Car Bombs and doesn't remember what happens between 9 a.m. and Noon, in which case that person is liberal. Unless, of course, that person comes to around 1:00 p.m. to find they're at a Qdoba with their friends, in which case that person is a Dublin dunce, and they'll be ferrying across the River Styx with no return ticket! BUT! If that person wants to head downtown to keep drinking and their friends won't let them so that person sprints to a taxi and hops in, heads downtown, and then wanders around downtown for about an hour until they bump into their friends at a pub called Flogging Molly, in which case they are a leprechaun's leftover, and they'll be boiling in the pot at the end of the inferno's rainbow! The one exception is that if the person ends up going back to their friend's apartment and does a few shots of Jameson's before ordering two pizzas from a pizza place called *Onomotopizza* where you get free breadsticks if you say "Mmmmmmmmm" when you order but they pass out before the pizzas come and wake up around midnight with the Pogues's "Stremas of Whiskey" blaring on repeat and all the pizza from *Onomotopizza* is gone but there's a note on the box that says "We're at James Joyce's," (which isn't James Joyce's house but a bar down the block from your apartment) and the person gets up and goes to James Joyce's, then that person is conservative.

If a person is a bartender at an Irish pub and wears a giant foam Guinness hat all day through their double shift and good naturedly tolerates people grabbing their hat and putting in on their own heads for pictures and so forth and then, at the end of the night, sells the hat to a drunk person who pays them $250 for it, that person is one lucky bastard...who will soon be pouring draughts for demons if they don't pray for forgiveness at the foot of the cross.

How to Tell Whether Someone is Liberal or Conservative on the 4th of July

If someone's go-to 4th of July song is Springsteen's "Born in the USA," they're conservative.

If their go-to 4th of July song is "American Tune" by Simon & Garfunkel, they're liberal.

If it's "This is America" by Childish Gambino, they're liberal and they're not celebrating.

If a man is wearing a graphic tee with George Washington riding a bald eagle while wielding an AK-47, he's conservative, but if the shirt features Ulysses S Grant punching a bear in the face he's liberal.

If a woman is wearing oversized red, white, or blue sunglasses she's conservative. If the sunglasses are undersized, she's liberal.

If a man is wearing a Pepsi-bezel Rolex GMT (the red and blue one with the obnoxiously big bubble on the date) he's conservative. However, if a woman is wearing the same watch she's liberal. It's rare but not unheard of for them to be married to each other.

If the party features a tie-dye station, the crowd is 89% liberal.

If the party features a wet T-shirt contest, the crowd is 99% conservative.

If the party devolves into a Roman Candle fight, the crowd is split 50-50.

If the party features a "Beer Olympics" between several groups of 17-year-olds in culturally offensive costumes, the parents are probably conservative but definitely out of town.

If someone's favorite firework is the streamer that fizzles out at the end, they're liberal.

If someone's favorite firework is "the big one," they're conservative.

If someone prefers drone shows, they're liberal. Unless they operate the drones.

Then they're very conservative.

If someone can name more people who have won the Nathan's Famous Hot Dog Eating Contest than they can people who signed the Declaration of Independence, they are a discouraging example of our nation's ego. However, we're also impressed and would like to meet this person.

If someone thinks the Nathan's Famous Hot Dog Eating Contest is gross, they're liberal. If someone has competed in or won the Nathan's Famous Hot Dog Eating Contest, they're conservative.

If someone was born on the 4th of July, they're conservative whether they like it or not.

How to Tell if Someone is Liberal or Conservative at the Oscars

If someone is at the Oscars, they are liberal.

How to Tell if Someone is Liberal or Conservative at the Daytona 500

If someone is at the Daytona 500, they are conservative.

What a Person's Favorite Valentine's Day Movie Says About What They Think is the Most Pressing Problem in America Today

Movie	Issue
Casablanca (1942)	Inflation, but only when purchasing vintage aircraft in North African markets
Pride and Prejudice (2005)	Health care affordability and whether rare 19th-century ailments like scurvy would be considered pre-existing conditions under your existing plan
La La Land (2016)	Violent crime, assuming it's directly related to disputes over jazz music royalties
Amélie (2001)	The state of moral values of whimsical Parisian waitresses
Titanic (1997)	Illegal immigration, Jack Dawson sneaking into the first-class dining areas was a significant breach of the rigid class barriers of the era. His intrusion into this elite space was both daring and unsettling and caused many great discomfort. Also, I was aghast when Jack Dawson drew those nude sketches of Rose. He defied the conservative norms of the early 20th century and challenged the propriety expected of a young woman of Rose's social standing.
Before Sunrise (1995)	Climate change, assuming you're discussing the impact on European train travel.

Movie	Issue
The Natural (1984)	The biggest problem in America? It's Major League Baseball's pitching crisis. Major League Baseball is facing a crisis with the increasing number of pitchers suffering significant arm injuries. Recent cases include Nationals' Josiah Gray and Red Sox's Nick Pivetta. The trend is attributed to various factors, including the introduction of the pitch clock, increased velocity, and spin rates. The MLB Players Association and the commissioner's office are at odds over the causes, with no clear solution in sight. Notable pitchers like Gerrit Cole and Noah Syndergaard have faced similar issues, emphasizing the need for the sport to address these injuries to preserve the game's integrity and player health.
West Side Story (1961)	Racism, but only within the dynamics of New York City's rival dance gangs
Eternal Sunshine of the Spotless Mind (2004)	State of roads and bridges, especially if considering the infrastructure of memory-laden landscapes
Pride & Prejudice (1995, TV)	Domestic terrorism, but only related to historical disputes over English estates
Beauty and the Beast (1991)	International terrorism, especially if such terrorism threatens the security of enchanted French castles
Sense and Sensibility (1995)	Unemployment, but only among genteel, landless gentry in 18th-century England
Sleepless in Seattle (1993)	Health care affordability, especially when dealing with sleep disorders in major U.S. cities
When Harry Met Sally (1989)	State of moral values, but only as such values pertain to women enjoying themselves in NYC diners or just enjoying themselves in general
Dirty Dancing (1987)	Abortion, but only during dance training at upscale Catskills resorts or when your mistress needs to have one
The English Patient (1996)	Violent crime, especially in the deserts of North Africa during WWII
Notting Hill (1999)	Federal budget deficit, but only in relation to subsidies for British bookshops
Love Actually (2003)	The quality of public schools, but only when considering the British education system around Christmas
The Shape of Water (2017)	Climate change, especially if assessing the ecological impact on half human half amphibious creatures
Doctor Zhivago (1965)	Racism, but only as it pertains to Eurasian conflicts in the early 20th century

Movie	Issue
Silver Linings Playbook (2012)	Domestic terrorism, and by "domestic terrorism" I mean the terror we all feel when we see Philadelphia sports fanaticism in action
Call Me by Your Name (2017)	International terrorism, especially if it means I have to cancel my trip to Italy
A Star Is Born (2018)	Unemployment, assuming it's in the Los Angeles entertainment industry
Wuthering Heights (1939)	Inflation, but only when dealing with the economics of isolated Yorkshire farms
Ghost (1990)	Illegal immigration, especially when it involves posthumous dead people illegally immigrating back to earth to talk to Molly.
Carol (2015)	Smoking in restaurants, remember how cool this used to be? Let's bring back smoking in restaurants
The Great Gatsby (2013)	Corporate greed, if you're always rationalizing the income disparity of today with "that's how it's always been"

How to Tell Whether Someone is Liberal or Conservative at a Bachelor Party

If the party involves golf, the bachelor is conservative.

If the party involves hiking, the bachelor is liberal.

If the party involves a shooting range, everyone is conservative.

If the party involves cabaret, everyone is liberal.

If someone in Cabo throws up after their first shot of tequila, they're in for a long weekend.

If someone in Cabo throws up after their first cup of water, they're in for a much longer weekend.

If someone in Nashville knows the words to every song being played at the bars, they're conservative.

If someone can do the same thing but the party is in Lake Tahoe, they're liberal.

If, while skiing in Park City, someone jokes about how this may be the last time they'll all get to ski together before global warming melts away the snow forever, they're liberal.

If, while surfing in Costa Rica, someone jokes about how annoying it is that the local government won't sell waterfront property to Americans, they're conservative.

If, while clubbing in Miami, someone [REDACTED] in front of [REDACTED] while [REDACTED], they're liberal.

If, while boating in Austin, someone [REDACTED] from the [REDACTED] while [REDACTED] and [REDACTED] both throw a football at [REDACTED], they're conservative.

If, while gambling in Las Vegas, someone [REDACTED] at the Aria only to find out the rest of the gang is [REDACTED] with [REDACTED] back at the MGM, so he rushes out only to [REDACTED] a security guard by accident and eventually [REDACTED] a [REDACTED] in prison, he was liberal before the trip but will likely be conservative the rest of his life.

If everyone gets matching boxing glove tattoos, they're awesome.

How to Tell Whether Someone is Liberal or Conservative at Weddings

If a man wears a black suit and tie even though the dress code says "cocktail attire," he's conservative.

If a woman wears a pantsuit even though the dress code says "cowboy chic," she's liberal.

If the bridesmaids all have matching Lily Pulitzer dresses, the bride is conservative.

If the groomsmen all have matching bolo ties, the groom is liberal. If the groom is the only one wearing a bolo tie, he's conservative.

If a woman stores airplane bottles of Jack Daniel's in her clutch for the ceremony, she's conservative.

If the bottles are of José Cuervo, she's liberal. (Unless her clutch is a sequined Confederate Flag, in which case she's still conservative),

If they're of Jägermeister, she just went through a breakup. And her ex is there.

If, at any point during the processional, someone loudly calls the groom by an old nickname like "Scooter" or "Fartbag" or "Meathead" or "Oil Can" or "Rambo," they are conservative.

If a man incorrectly tells you who composed the recessional tune, he's probably liberal. If he's correct though, he's definitely conservative.

If the wedding is in July and a man still orders the beef tenderloin for dinner, he's conservative.

If the wedding is in January and he orders the fish, he's liberal.

If a man you haven't seen in 10 years offers you a bump of coke in the bathroom, he's conservative.

If he offers you mushrooms, he's liberal.

If the father of the bride quotes Ernest Hemingway in his speech, he's conservative.

If he quotes Kurt Vonnegut, he's liberal.

If he quotes the Dali Lama, he googled "Dad wedding speech" that morning.

If the best man and maid of honor treat their speeches like a duet, where the jokes play off each other, they are definitely hooking up later.

If two guests get in a fight after drinking too many John Dalys, one is liberal and the other is conservative. Unless they fight over the bouquet. Then they're both just desperate.

If the wedding party dances up the aisle to Chris Brown's "Forever," it's 2009.

If anyone even thinks the word "divorce," they need to keep it to themselves.

If anyone brings finger guns to the dance floor, they're liberal.

If they bring real guns, they're conservative.

If a person marries someone of Polish descent and that person's parents practice the polka in their garage before the wedding, the person getting married is, was, and always will be liberal and the parents were conservative once but grew tired of ... just the whole thing ... and are now liberal AF.

If someone cries during "Dancing Queen" they are liberal.

If someone cries during "Brown Eyed Girl" they are conservative.

If someone doesn't cry during "You Send Me," something is wrong with them.

If, during the reception when the DJ plays "Cotton Eye Joe" by Rednex, someone bumps into your great aunt and your great aunt dislocates her knee, the person who bumped into her is conservative.

If, during the reception when the DJ plays "Cotton Eye Joe" by Rednex, someone bumps into your great aunt and your great aunt sprains her ankle, the person who bumped into her is liberal.

If, at the end of the reception when the band plays "Shout!" and everyone is trying to get as low as they possibly can to the floor without actually lying down, a man accidentally slips and it causes a domino effect that knocks everyone over—even the bride's grandma—that man is liberal. (Don't ask how we know this.)

How to Tell Whether Someone is Liberal or Conservative at a Funeral

If a bereaved man greets you with a solemn two-handed handshake, he's conservative.

If he greets you with a solemn hug, he's liberal.

If a bereaved woman greets you with a cold shoulder, she remembers what you said about Tom after a few drinks at Alice's house in '09.

If she greets you with a slap to the face, she knows what you did, even if the cops don't.

If the priest/ rabbi/shaman is younger than the deceased, they're liberal. If they're older, they're conservative.

If a eulogizer jokes that "He's survived by three children: His son Sam, his daughter Caroline, and his bicycle Bentley," the deceased was liberal.

If a eulogizer jokes that, "He loved golf, but golf did not love him back," the deceased was conservative.

If the organist plays "When the Saints Go Marching In" by the book, they're conservative. If they add a little personal flare, especially in those opening notes, they're liberal.

If a pallbearer is wearing a lapel pin of the deceased's favorite baseball team, he's conservative. If they're wearing a "Bongs Over Bombs" pin from his and the deceased's activist days, he's liberal.

If the toughest-looking guy in the room is crying the hardest, he's never been this vulnerable in his whole life. Give him a hug already.

If the softest-looking guy in the room is crying the hardest, he's used to being this vulnerable, but he still deserves a hug.

If there are two detectives in the back whispering to each other, one is liberal and one is conservative. We can't tell which is which though.

If there's a small woman sitting alone in the middle row with mysterious ties to the deceased, the detectives think she's the killer but she's not.

If there's a tall woman sitting with a short man who knew the deceased "from an old job," they're defiitely the killers.

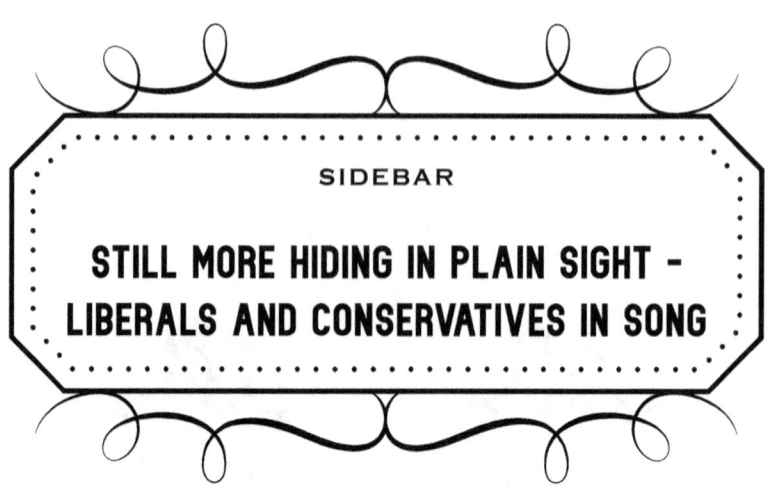

STILL MORE HIDING IN PLAIN SIGHT – LIBERALS AND CONSERVATIVES IN SONG

Stacy's Mom

Analyzing Stacy's mom from the iconic tune "Stacy's Mom" by Fountains of Wayne reveals intriguing insights into the titular character's political leanings. The song's catchy chorus and vivid storytelling paint Stacy's mom as an emblem of conservative values, albeit in an unconventional manner.

Firstly, something is wrong with Stacy's mom. Seriously lady get it together. But then, Stacy's mom's allure, encapsulated in the line, "Stacy's mom has got it going on," subtly hints at a traditional appeal and timeless charm that often resonate with conservative ideals. Her ability to captivate attention while ostensibly maintaining a classic suburban lifestyle suggests a nod to conservative virtues of family values and the allure of the familiar. Furthermore, the fact that Stacy's mom was on a business trip, as evinced in the very first verse indicate that she works. Working is something that very few liberals do. Conservatives do all the working. Therefore Stacy's mom is a conservative. Moreover, the setting of the song, with its quintessentially suburban backdrop, complete with "the car up the street," evokes a sense of Americana that is often romanticized in conservative narratives. Stacy's mom, as the central figure in this setting, becomes a symbol of the enduring charm and stability of suburban American life.

Jessie

Rick Springfield's "Jessie's Girl" is a tale of longing and unrequited love, set to an infectious beat that defined an era. Through the lens of this classic pop-rock anthem, it's clear that Jessie, the object of the narrator's envy, embodies conservative values, particularly in the context of relationships and personal conduct and the fact that he possesses his girl.

The song's narrative centers around the narrator's desire for the girl who, by virtue of the apostrophe after his name, belongs to Jessie. Jessie's qualities make him an enviable partner. Lyrics like, "And she's loving him with that body, I just know it," and "You know, I feel so dirty when they start talking cute," suggest Jessie's relationship is built on a foundation of mutual respect and attraction, qualities often championed by conservative views on romantic relationships. And again, that apostrophe "s" indicates that he owns her. In an Amy Coney Barrett kind of way.

Jessie's ability to maintain a committed and desirable relationship, coupled with the narrator's yearning for such stability and fidelity, reflects conservative ideals of monogamy, loyalty, and the sanctity of romantic commitments. The song portrays Jessie as a man who has successfully navigated the complexities of love to build a relationship that others admire, embodying conservative principles of dedication and personal responsibility in matters of the heart. Like when Matt Gaetz hires an underage sex worker, he takes personal responsibility for her. Moreover, the song's focus on the emotional turmoil of wanting what one cannot have speaks to the conservative virtue of self-restraint and the importance of respecting the boundaries of others' relationships, even in the face of deep personal longing.

Roxanne

The Police's "Roxanne" is a compelling narrative set against a reggae-infused rock backdrop. It tells the story of a woman caught in the red lights of life's darker streets. Through the song's poignant lyrics and emotive delivery, it's clear that Roxanne, despite her circumstances, embodies liberal ideals, particularly in terms of personal agency and societal empathy.

The chorus, "Roxanne, you don't have to put on the red light," is a plea for Roxanne to see beyond her current situation, hinting at the liberal value of personal freedom and the belief in one's capacity to change their life path - with nary any indicia of bootstraps. The song's narrator recognizes Roxanne's autonomy and urges her to make choices not constrained by the expectations or judgments of society.

Furthermore, the song's empathetic stance towards Roxanne's plight reflects a liberal emphasis on understanding and compassion for those in less fortunate circumstances. Rather than passing judgment, the song seeks to offer support and a way out, embodying the liberal ideal of lifting others up and advocating for social justice and equity. Additionally, the song's narrative invites listeners to consider the broader social and economic factors that lead individuals like Roxanne to the choices they make, encouraging a liberal-leaning discourse on systemic change and the need for societal compassion and understanding.

Part Five -

ALL OVER THE U.S.A.

How to Tell If Someone is Liberal or Conservative in Boston.

If a person's favorite Aerosmith song is "Dream On," that person is a liberal.

If a person's favorite Aerosmith song is "Janie's Got a Gun," that person is a conservative.

If a person's favorite Aerosmith song is "I Don't Want to Miss a Thing," get that person's contact information. The next time an asteroid is heading towards Earth and you need someone to fly to space, drill a hole in the asteroid, and plant a thermonuclear device, this person could come in handy.

If a person has ever smoked a pipe with Henry Cabot Lodge or his progeny in a Ropes & Gray conference room, that person is a conservative.

If a person has ever smoked anything with Evan Dando in Harvard Square, that person is a liberal.

If a blue-collar-looking man is outside of a Dunkin Donuts in Harvard Square asking a well-dressed man inside the Dunkin Donuts if he likes apples, that blue-collar man is Will Hunting, he just got Skylar's number, and you wouldn't know it by looking at him, but that man is a genius.

If you are on the outbound "B" train of the Green Line, headed to a party on Cinco de Mayo, and a girl gets on the "T" carrying a tray of Tequila Sunrise Jell-O shots, the girl carrying those Jell-O shots is liberal.

If on that same outbound "B" train of the Green Line, another woman gets on the "T" and karate chops that tray of Tequila Sunrise Jell-O shots so that they go flying everywhere, the woman who did the karate chopping is a liberal.

If on that same outbound "B" train of the Green Line, people scurry about the "T" car looking for the spilled Tequila Sunrise Jell-o shots so they can do the Jell-O shot, those people are all liberal.

If the driver of that same outbound "B" train of the Green Line, stops the train and uses the Green Line's PA system to talk about cultural appropriation, that T conductor is a liberal.

If your significant other graduates from one of Boston's 44 colleges or universities with a nursing degree, you should have a graduation party for them and make Jell-o shots but put the Jell-o shots in syringes. You'll need to add more alcohol that your Jell-o shot recipe calls for so the Jell-o can squeeze out of the syringe with ease. But that would be a fun way to celebrate the new nurse in your life!

If a person craves the New England Clam Chowder from Union Oyster House, that person is a liberal.

If you are in the Massachusetts State House and see a person with the best hair you have ever seen eating a hot dog and it's sometime between 2003 and 2007, that person is Mitt Romney.

If a person stops at Dunkin on their way to a Bruins game and you are in the Dunkin too and you look at that person wrong, you are about to get the shit kicked out of you.

If you see a person eating Boston baked beans from the Beantown Pub, you should not sit next to that person on the T.

If a person was once in the Tufts Beelzebubs, that person is a liberal.

If a person believes that Beelzebub's return is nigh, that person is either a conservative or the ghost of someone actively involved in the Salem witch trials.

If a person has read Jack Kerouac's On the Road more than once, that person is a liberal.

If a person has worn red pants to Jack Welch's house on Nantucket, that person is a conservative.

If a person is driving a truck with at least one wheel missing through Allston and you can see sparks from where the rim is hitting the asphalt, the person driving that truck is neither a liberal nor a conservative, he is just a person from Allston.

If a person buys rollerblades and rollerblades down the Esplanade, that person is a conservative. Unless that person was rollerblading down the Esplanade on September 9, 1994, in which case that person is likely a survivor of the Green Day riot at the Hatch Shell and therefore likely a liberal.

If a person puts tomato on their lobster roll, that person is a conservative.

If a person wearing red leather pants is grinding their loins on a pole in a car of the Orange Line of the T while listening to Bjork's "Big Time Sensuality," that person is a liberal.

If a person wearing a fleece vest with "Wellington Management" embroidered on it is grinding their loins on a pole in a car of the Orange Line of the T while listening to Daft Punk's "One More Time" that person is a conservative.

If a person is wearing a black mohair sweater, buys a croissant from the Au Bon Pain at South Station, and spends the day with croissant crumbs stuck in their sweater, that person is a conservative. The kind of conservative who will never let you forget your religion.

How to Tell if Someone is Liberal or Conservative in New York City

This one time, we were riding the New York City (NYC) subway when we saw a lady inadvertently step on a rat scurrying across the subway platform. The lady was wearing the Christian Louboutin "So Kate[11]" black patent calf leather heels and its 120 mm heel stabbed the rat right through its fat, pizza-fed guts. The rat, though impaled on the heel of this lady's shoe, was still clearly alive, eerily recalling that 1800's railroad foreman Phineas Gage[12]. The

---

11   The So Kate iconic pump with timeless elegance brilliantly combines discretion and sophistication. Its all-black patent calfskin features a sculpted upper that extends its lines to the iconic bold cut. It sits easy atop a slender 120 mm heel to give you confidence, underlining Maison Christian Louboutin know-how.

12   In 1848, Phineas Gage, a 25-year-old railroad construction foreman, experienced a harrowing accident that became a landmark case in neuroscience. While working in Cavendish, Vermont, Gage was using a tamping iron to pack explosive powder into a hole. Unexpectedly, the powder detonated, propelling the 3-foot-7-inch, 13-pound iron rod through Gage's left cheek, piercing his brain, and exiting his skull. Miraculously, Gage survived the accident, but his personality underwent profound changes, offering early evidence of the brain's role in determining personality and behavior. Once known for his hardworking and pleasant demeanor, Gage became irreverent, impulsive, and had difficulty adhering to social norms post-accident. His story fascinated the medical community and the public alike, shedding light on the brain's complexity and its influence on human identity. Gage's life, drastically altered by a moment's event, continues to intrigue and inform neuroscience and psychology to this day.

rat was screaming[13] and it was clear that the lady on whose heel the rat clung was annoyed but by no means distressed. She then expertly and nonchalantly and flawlessly flung her leg in such a manner so that the rat was wrested from the heel of her Louboutin, was hurtled through the air and over the heads of the subway riders (who nonchalantly ducked), landed on the electrified third rail of the subway tracks, and sizzled to its death. The rodent's sizzling demise simultaneously recalled the wicked witch's melty death from *The Wizard of Oz*, Arnold Toht's melty face death in *Raiders of the Lost Ark*, and Jack Dawson's demise in *Titanic* in equal measure. The lady did this without spilling any of her coffee or losing her place in the article she was reading in that morning's *New York Times* and this must have been a Thursday because I recall she was reading "The Hunt." We determined that such a lady defied political pigeonholing and was quite simply, just...a New Yorker[14].

---

13 Who knew rats could scream? I didn't.

14 New York City's subway system serves as a unique microcosm of the city's broader social and cultural diversity, creating a shared space where individuals from various backgrounds interact daily. Reese and Gary have determined that the constant intermingling and coexistence fostered within the confines of the subway system contribute to the development of empathy among New Yorkers, which in turn, may predispose the city's residents towards more liberal political leanings.

The NYC subway system is one of the most extensive public transportation systems globally, facilitating over 1.7 billion rides annually. It connects disparate neighborhoods, from the affluent Upper East Side to the vibrant, multicultural boroughs of Queens and Brooklyn, making it a crossroads of the city's diverse population. Within the subway cars, bankers sit next to street artists, and students share space with immigrants from every corner of the globe. This daily, unavoidable interaction with the "other" serves as a constant reminder of the city's diversity, challenging preconceived notions and prejudices.

Empirical studies suggest that increased exposure to diversity can enhance social empathy, as individuals become more aware of and sensitive to different cultural and socioeconomic experiences. The subway, in its function as a public space where diverse groups coalesce, naturally cultivates this empathy. As empathy grows, so does support for inclusive, equitable policies that characterize liberal ideologies. Furthermore, the shared experience of navigating the subway's challenges, from delays to overcrowding to encountering a disguised Jimmy Fallon and U2 playing "I Still Haven't Found What I'm Looking For," fosters a sense of communal resilience and solidarity. This shared struggle not only strengthens the social fabric but also aligns with liberal values that emphasize community support and collective action.

In conclusion, the NYC subway system plays a pivotal role in promoting diversity and empathy among its riders. This daily exposure to the city's rich tapestry of life contributes to a communal environment where liberal political leanings are not only fostered but also thrive.

How to Tell if Someone is Liberal or Conservative in Seattle

The Rain Gear Fashionista. With a wardrobe that boasts an array of raincoats and waterproof boots, they turn dreary days into a fashion runway. Likely liberal, because they understand the importance of climate adaptation.

The Pike Place Performer. Whether they're tossing fish or serenading tourists with a guitar, these entertainers keep the market lively. Their political views? As diverse as their performances.

The Grunge Scene Veteran. Clad in flannel with tales from the '90s music scene, they mourn the days when Nirvana ruled the airwaves. Their politics? Apathetically anarchist.

The Mount Rainier Worshipper. On clear days, they're the first to point out the mountain's beauty. Their weekend plans always involve hiking or skiing. Conservatively speaking, they just want to preserve nature's splendor.

The Craft Beer Critic. With a discerning palate and a vocabulary filled with terms like "hop-forward" and "malty," they're on a perpetual quest for the perfect brew. Likely liberal, given their appreciation for diversity—in beers, at least.

Jeff Ament, Stone Gossard, Mike McCready, Eddie Vedder, and Matt Cameron. Liberal.

The Eco-Warrior Cyclist. They navigate the city on two wheels, rain or shine, advocating for sustainable transportation. Political leaning? Green, with a capital G.

The Space Needle Selfie King/Queen. Tourists? Maybe. Or just locals who still marvel at the iconic skyline. Regardless, they're snapping away, capturing every angle. Politically neutral, too busy editing their photos.

The Caffeine Connoisseur. These individuals know their coffee better than their family tree. They can distinguish between beans with their eyes closed and have a PhD in latte art. Political leaning? Too caffeinated to care.

The Tech Devotee. Found in the wild with the latest gadget in hand, they're probably conceptualizing an app as we speak. Often spotted in South Lake Union, their political leanings are as complex as their code.

The Tech Titan. This is where things get complicated. Once, we could count on these guys to be staunchly, vocally, and emphatically liberal. That whole income inequality thing though...

The Seahawks Superfan. Decked out in blue and green, they live and breathe football. Their loyalty to the team is unwavering, much like their conservative values—stick with what you know.

The Start-Up Maverick. Armed with a laptop and a dream, they're the future moguls of Seattle. Political leanings? Libertarian, because who needs regulations when you have innovation?

The Urban Farmer. Their backyard is a kaleidoscope of edible plants, and they're on a first-name basis with every chicken at the local farmers market. Politically liberal, in a grassroots kind of way.

The Ferry Frequent Flyer. They find solace in the rhythm of the waves and have mastered the art of the weekend island getaway. Political stance? Fluid, like the Puget Sound.

The Alki Beach Bum. Summer or not, they're soaking up the rays and playing beach volleyball. Their politics are laid-back, much like their beach attire.

The Underground Tour Guide. Full of historical tidbits about Seattle's subterranean past, they revel in the city's hidden stories. Their political leanings are as layered as the city's underground.

The Sushi Aficionado. They've got the inside scoop on the best rolls in town and aren't afraid to splurge on omakase. Politically? Progressive, with a taste for cultural exploration.

The Indie Bookshop Dweller. Lost in the labyrinth of shelves, they emerge only to attend the latest book reading. Likely liberal, fueled by a love of diverse narratives.

The Paddleboard Pioneer. Come rain or shine, they're out on the water, finding balance amidst the waves. Their political stance? Equally balanced, appreciating all perspectives.

The Amazonian. Not from the rainforest, but possibly just as exotic, they're reshaping the city's landscape one Prime delivery at a time. Their politics? Efficient, much like their shopping habits.

Ken Jennings. The smartest man in the history of *Jeopardy!* is liberal.

The Dog Park Socialite. Their canine companion is their ticket to the social whirlwind of Seattle's dog parks. Politically? *Bi-paw-tisan,* of course.

The Glass Art Enthusiast. Mesmerized by Chihuly's creations, they're advocates for Seattle's vibrant art scene. Liberal, with an appreciation for the fluidity of both glass and ideas.

The Thrift Store Treasure Hunter. With an eye for vintage finds, they turn secondhand shopping into a high fashion endeavor. Political leanings? Progressive, with a penchant for recycling.

The Emerald City Cosplayer. From comic cons to game expos, they bring fantasy to life with intricate costumes. Their politics? As varied as their cosplay characters.

The Greenlake Jogger. Rain or shine, they're lapping the lake, fueled by the city's love for outdoor fitness. Political stance? Running towards a more inclusive society.

The Salmon Savant. Whether they're fishing, cooking, or just eating, they're passionate about the Pacific Northwest's favorite fish. Their political views? Fluid, like the rivers they fish in.

How to Tell is Someone is Liberal or Conservative in Baltimore

The Crabber. This individual's idea of a perfect meal involves a mallet, a pile of Old Bay-seasoned crabs, and a bib. Their political stance? As balanced as their spice-to-meat ratio.

The Hon. Sporting beehive hairdos and bright, vintage dresses, they keep the quirky spirit of Baltimore alive. Likely liberal, with a flair for retro fashion and progressive ideals.

The Natty Boh Connoisseur. Clutching a National Bohemian Beer, they're the embodiment of local loyalty. Their political views are as straightforward as their choice of brew—no frills, just the basics.

That Guy in the Ray Lewis Jersey. They wear their Ravens gear with pride, rain or shine, game day or not. Political leaning? Defensive, especially if you criticize their team.

The Inner Harborist. Whether they're a tourist or a local rediscovering the waterfront, they can't get enough of the scenic views. Politically neutral, too enchanted by the harbor's charm.

The Parker Posey. These people are among the few that know Parkey Posey was born in Baltimore on November 8, 1968. They have a unique blend of wit, charm, nuance, and depth. They are independent, just like Parker Posey's films, and eager to see the Inner Harbor leveled to become "Parker Posey Plaza."

The Edgar Allan Poe Devotee. With a deep appreciation for the macabre, they can recite "The Raven" by heart. Likely a liberal goth, with a penchant for the poetic and the eerie. (Note: Not to be confused with the "Poe Toaster," who, starting in 1949 and for more than half a century thereafter, visited Edgar Allan Poe's gravesite on the eve of his birthday, January 19, every year. The Poe Toaster, who to this day remains anonymous, left a partial bottle of cognac along with three roses at the site. That individual defies categorization.)

The Berger Cookie Baker. A master of the local delicacy, their cookies are a hit at every gathering. Their politics are as sweet and complex as their chocolate-topped treats.

The John Waters. Their political leanings? "I'll get you pussy face!!!" Need we say more?

The Fells Point Pirate. Arrrrggh. On weekends, they're exploring the cobblestone streets of Fells Point, possibly in full pirate regalia during festivals. Political stance? Anarchical, marine biological, nautical, with a love for maritime lawlessness.

The Preakness Patron. Dressed to the nines for the races, they're all about the tradition and the thrill of the bet. Conservative, perhaps, with a gamble. (Not to be confused with the people in the infield who "run the port a potties." Google it.)

The ArtScapist. Immersed in Baltimore's annual arts festival, they're either showcasing their work or admiring others'. Liberal, with a canvas as colorful as their views.

The Johns Hopkins Scholar. With their nose in a book or lost in groundbreaking research, they're shaping the future one discovery at a time. Political leanings? Academically liberal, questioning everything.

The Lexington Market Foodie. They know where to get the best of everything, from fresh seafood to international delicacies. Politically open-minded, with a palate as diverse as Baltimore itself.

The Commuter. Live in Baltimore so they can work in DC. Likely centrist, valuing both sides of the spectrum.

The Rowhouse Renovator. They see the potential in every historic home, dedicated to preserving Charm City's architectural heritage. Political stance? Conservative, in a preservationist sort of way.

The Harbor East Elite. With a taste for the finer things, they frequent the upscale shops and restaurants of Harbor East. Their politics? Privately liberal, publicly nonchalant.

The Michael Phelps. These people swim so fast that we haven't yet been able to ask them about their political ideologies.

The Orioles Optimist. Ever hopeful for the Orioles' return to glory, their team spirit never wanes. Political leaning? Optimistically bipartisan, believing in the power of whichever candidates don't stand a chance.

The Water Taxi Rider. Preferring the scenic route, they navigate the city via its waterways. Politically fluid, they go with the flow.

The Spiro Agnew. These Baltimoreans are known for their outspoken conservative viewpoints and their constant critiques of the media and anti-war demonstrators. They are often investigated on charges of extortion, tax fraud, bribery, and conspiracy.

The Mount Vernon Local. Living amidst the historical and cultural heart of Baltimore, they're always up for a museum visit or a concert. Liberal, with a love for community and culture.

The MICA Visionary. A student or alum of the Maryland Institute College of Art, they're the future of creativity. Politically progressive, pushing boundaries in art and life.

The Patterson Park Jogger. They find their zen running past the pagoda and duck pond, embracing the city's green spaces. Political stance? Green party, in a literal and figurative sense.

The Evangelist. They'll teach anyone the art of eating Maryland's signature dish, steamed crabs, and turn crustacean skeptics into shellfish believers. Politically, they're inclusive, with a "more the merrier" attitude.

The Hampden Hipster. With a love for the quirky and the independent, they thrive in Baltimore's most eclectic neighborhood. Politically left-leaning, with a penchant for artisanal everything.

How to Tell if Someone is Liberal or Conservative in Buffalo

The Wing King/Queen. They've got strong opinions on who makes the best Buffalo wings in town and aren't afraid to debate it. Political leaning? Spicy, with a side of blue cheese.

The Sculptor. When winter hits, they see a canvas, not a chore. Their driveway is less "cleared" and more "curated." Likely liberal, creatively turning problems into art.

The Bills Mafia Member. Tailgating is their religion, and they worship at the altar of the Buffalo Bills. Will they tell you in detail about how their mom's best friend's daughter is Jim Kelly's neighbor's dental hygienist? Yes. Will they show you their Bills tattoos? Yes. Did they get married wearing Bills attire, take pictures at the stadium, and cut a Bills-themed wedding cake? Yes. Can they tell you wear they were on January 3, 1993 even if

they weren't born yet? Yes. Their political stance? Loyal, with a readiness to jump through tables for their beliefs.

The Eternal Optimist. They've seen the city's ups and downs and believe in its comeback story. Their politics? Optimistically bipartisan, rooting for the underdog.

The Dyngus Day Devotee. Come Easter Monday, they're armed with a water gun and a pussywillow branch, embracing this unique Polish tradition.

Politically? Inclusive, with a penchant for fun.

The Goo Goo Doll. Is "Iris" from the City of Angels soundtrack the greatest song ever recorded besides "Name," track six from the 1995 masterpiece A Boy Named Goo? Yes. Political leanings? Could you whisper in my ear the things you wanna feel?

The Beef on Weck Connoisseur. They know the best spots for this Buffalo delicacy and will judge you for using too much horseradish. Political stance? Conservative, in a culinary sense.

The Elmwood Village Artist. From art festivals to local galleries, they're all about the vibrant arts scene in Buffalo. Likely liberal, painting the town with broad strokes of diversity.

The Blizzard Braver. They wear shorts in snowstorms and consider anything less than a foot of snow "a dusting." Political leaning? Stoic, with a resilience that's weatherproof.

The Larkinville Luncher. Enjoying the food trucks and live music, they're a regular at Larkin Square's events. Politically, they're community-oriented, valuing local eats and beats.

The Allentown Advocate. This person loves the quirky, historic charm of Allentown and supports its eclectic mix of businesses. Liberal, appreciating the neighborhood's diverse and inclusive vibe.

The Sabres Superfan. Winter means hockey season, and they bleed blue and gold for the Buffalo Sabres. Their politics? Defensive, especially when it comes to defending their team.

The Parkside Preservationist. Living in one of Buffalo's picturesque historic districts is about preserving its architectural beauty. Likely conservative, with a love for heritage and history.

The Silo City Explorer. Fascinated by Buffalo's industrial past, they're always ready for a tour of the grain elevators. Political stance? Progressive, seeing potential in the city's relics.

The Niagara Frontier Naturalist. They spend their weekends exploring the region's parks and waterfalls, advocating for the environment. Likely liberal, with a green thumb and a green heart.

The Anchor Bar Regular. Claiming loyalty to the birthplace of the Buffalo wing, they're a fixture at the iconic bar. Political leaning? Traditional, with a side of historical pride.

The Richardson Olmsted Campus Wanderer. Enthralled by the history and architecture, they always enjoy visiting this landmark site. Likely liberal, with an appreciation for preservation and mental health awareness.

The Taste of Buffalo Foodie. They plan their year around this festival, eager to sample all the local cuisine. Politically? Open-minded, with a palate for diversity.

The Shakespeare in Delaware Park Patron. Bringing their own lawn chair, they're devotees of Buffalo's summer tradition of free theater. They're likely liberal, believing in accessible art for all.

The Garden Walk Gardener. Proudly showcasing their urban oasis during Buffalo's annual Garden Walk, they have a green thumb and a community spirit. Politically green, nurturing nature and neighborhoods alike.

The Rust Belt Revivalist. They're all about celebrating and revitalizing Buffalo's industrial heritage, one reclaimed space at a time. Political stance? Progressive, with a DIY attitude.

The Hertel Avenue Hipster. Sipping craft coffee and scouting out vintage finds, they're a staple of this trendy strip. Likely liberal, with a taste for the artisanal and the authentic.

The Buffalo Zoo Zookeeper. Whether they work there or just visit often, they're passionate about animal conservation and education. Likely liberal, with a big heart for furry and feathered friends.

The Winter Festival Warrior. From ice biking to igloo dining, they embrace Buffalo's winter festivals with gusto. Political leaning? Adventurous, with a policy of embracing the cold.

The Peace Bridge Crosser. Regularly venturing to Canada for day trips, they embody the international spirit of the region. Politically? Diplomatic, with a passport full of stamps.

How to Tell if Someone is Liberal or Conservative in Miami

The South Beach Socialite. They live for the beach by day and the club by night, always dressed to impress. Political stance? Glamorously liberal, with a flair for the dramatic.

The Cafecito Connoisseur. They can't start their day without a Cuban coffee, and they have strong opinions on where to find the best one. Political leaning? Energized, with a shot of conservative tradition.

The Wynwood Wall Artist. With spray cans as their tools, they contribute to the ever-changing urban canvas of Wynwood. Likely liberal, with a passion for street art and social messages.

The Alligator Whisperer. They spend their weekends kayaking through the Everglades's mangroves spotting and talking to alligators, advocating for environmental preservation. Political stance? Green, in every sense of the word.

The Sonny Crockett. Like the iconic character from the hit 1980s television series "Miami Vice," this person epitomizes the cool and stylish undercover detective. They are charismatic and complex and navigate the dangerous and glamorous world of Miami's criminal underworld. They dressed in pastel suits, T-shirts, and loafers without socks. They drive a sleek Ferrari and live on a sailboat with an alligator named Elvis. Their lifestyle is as flamboyant as it is fraught with peril and their personal life is complicated, often blending into their professional world and leading to turbulent relationships and emotional struggles. They have a deep commitment to justice, a brooding introspection, and a penchant for bending the rules to achieve their ends. Political leanings? Look no further than what their namesake said in Season 1 episode 16: "People in stucco houses shouldn't throw quiche."

The Ricardo Tubbs. This person is suave and sophisticated and likely a New York City detective who ventured to Miami to avenge their brother's death. They have quickly becomes an integral part of the Miami Vice police unit. Their streetwise intelligence, sharp detective skills, and impeccable fashion sense—featuring sleek suits and a smooth, no-nonsense demeanor—bring a unique blend of northern grit and southern charm to the sun-drenched streets of Miami. They are driven by a strong moral compass and a personal quest for justice, often adding emotional depth and narrative complexity to personal and professional situations. They are perpetually cool and composed. Politically? Tubbs was a huuuuuuuge Keynesian and advocated for Keynesian economics, developed by John Maynard Keynes. Tubbs advocates for government intervention to manage economic cycles. Tubbs always suggested that during recessions, increased public spending and lower taxes can stimulate demand, reduce unemployment, and foster recovery, while in booms, the government should cut spending and increase taxes to cool the economy.

The Art Basel Regular. Each December, they're immersed in the world of contemporary art, mingling with artists and collectors alike. Politically? Progressive, with a taste for avant-garde.

The Calle Ocho Dancer. Salsa runs through their veins, and they're always ready to show off their moves at the drop of a hat. Likely liberal, celebrating the rhythm of Miami's multicultural beat.

The Luxury Yacht Lounger. Their idea of a perfect weekend involves sailing Miami's crystal waters on a yacht. Political leaning? Lavishly conservative, with a penchant for the finer things.

The Little Havana Historian. Passionate about Cuban culture and history, they're a walking encyclopedia on the area's heritage. Political stance? Nostalgically conservative, cherishing their roots.

The Coral Gables Gourmet. They have a refined palate and dine exclusively at the finest restaurants in The City Beautiful. Likely liberal, with a taste for international cuisines and cultures.

The Key Biscayne Kitesurfer. Harnessing the power of the wind, they're a regular on the water, chasing the ultimate thrill. Politically? Adventurous, with a free-spirited outlook.

The Miami Heat Die-Hard. Wearing their team colors with pride, they never miss a game and defend their team with fervor. Political stance? Fiery, with a competitive edge.

The Brickell Business Mogul. Clad in designer suits, they navigate the skyscrapers of Miami's financial district, always on the move. Likely conservative, with a focus on fiscal matters.

The Coconut Grove Bohemian. Amidst the lush greenery, they embrace a laid-back lifestyle, valuing community and simplicity. Politically? Liberal, with a love for organic living.

The Design District Aficionado. They appreciate the finer things in life, from luxury fashion to high-end furniture. Political leaning? Fashionably liberal, with an eye for aesthetics.

The Ultra Music Festival Raver. Each March, they live for the beats of this iconic electronic music festival, dancing until dawn. Likely liberal, with a pulse on the global music scene.

The Paddleboard Peacekeeper. Gliding through the calm waters of Biscayne Bay, they find their zen in the balance between city and sea. Political stance? Balanced, seeking harmony in all things.

The Mojito Connoisseur. Knows mojitos. Lives mojitos. Loves mojitos. Laughs at mojitos. Cries with mojitos. Political leaning? More mojitos please.

The Gloria Estefan. This person, is likely a trailblazing singer-songwriter who fled Cuba with their family as a child due to the Cuban Revolution. They grew up in Miami, where they absorbed diverse musical influences. Their breakthrough comes when they join a band led by a man they will marry later. Their fusion of pop with Cuban rhythms catapult them to international fame until a near-fatal bus accident forces them to start all over again. They make a remarkable comeback which underscores their resilience and passion for music. Politically? They are rhythmists because the rhythm is gonna get ya.

The Fisher Island Ferry Rider. Exclusive and elusive, they commute to one of Miami's most private communities by ferry. Political stance? Privately conservative, in a gated-community sort of way.

The MIMO Architecture Admirer. They have a keen eye for Miami's unique mid-century modern architectural style and are passionate about its preservation. Likely liberal, with a respect for historical aesthetics.

The Aventura Mall Maven. With a penchant for luxury, they frequent this upscale mall for their fashion and lifestyle needs. Political leaning? Chicly conservative, where style meets substance.

The Vizcaya Enthusiast. They're enchanted by the beauty and history of this lavish Italianate mansion and its gardens. Politically? Cultured, with a penchant for the opulent and the historic.

The Ocean Drive Night Owl. Thriving in the neon-lit nightlife of Miami Beach, they're a staple of the after-hours scene. Political stance? Liberally nocturnal, with a love for the city that never sleeps.

The Hurricane Season Prepper. With a well-stocked pantry and shutters at the ready, they're unfazed by the threat of storms. Political leaning? Pragmatically conservative, always prepared for the worst.

How to Tell if Someone is Liberal or Conservative in Chicago

The Oprah. They were one of the 276 people in the audience at Harpo studios on September 13, 2004. The day. The day to end all days. They still drive their Pontiac G-6 sedan. Politically? As liberal as a Pontiac G-6 sedan allows one to be.

The Deep-Dish Devotee. They have strong opinions on the best pizza in town and aren't afraid to debate it. Political leaning? Deeply conservative, in a crust-we-trust kind of way.

The Lakefront Runner. Come rain, shine, or snow, they're pounding the pavement along Lake Michigan's shore. Likely liberal, embracing the lake's open waters and open-mindedness.

The Second City Standout. Quick-witted and always ready for a laugh, they thrive in the world of improv comedy. Political stance? Improvisationally liberal, with a knack for thinking on their feet.

The Loyal Cubs Fan. Win or lose, they bleed Cubbie blue, with a resilience born from a century-long wait for a World Series win. Political leaning? Hopeful, with an undying loyalty to the underdog.

The James Iha. With their distinctive style and understated presence, these people contribute significantly to their respective bands' lush, layered sound. Politically? June bug skipping like a stone with the headlights pointed at the dawn.

The Magnificent Mile Shopper. From luxury brands to iconic department stores, they easily navigate this shopping paradise. They are likely conservative, with a taste for the finer things and the status quo.

The Art Institute Aficionado. They lose themselves in the galleries, finding peace among the masterpieces. Politically? Progressive, with a palette for diversity and expression.

The Bean Selfie Specialist. Every visit to Millennium Park requires a reflective selfie. Political stance? Reflective, capturing every moment from multiple angles.

The I Knew Obama When. These people knew Obama when. Liberal.

The Wrigleyville Warbler. Post-game, they're belting out tunes in the local bars, celebrating or commiserating in song. Likely liberal, finding camaraderie in communal sing-alongs.

The Chicago River Kayaker. They see the city from a different angle, paddling between the skyscrapers. Political leaning? Fluid, navigating the currents of change with ease.

The Willis Tower Skydeck Visitor. Fearlessly stepping onto the glass ledge, they relish the thrill of hovering 1,353 feet above the ground. Politically? Vertically liberal, embracing lofty views and ideas.

The Green City Market Patron. Every Saturday, they're sourcing the freshest local produce, committed to sustainable eating. Likely liberal, with a green thumb and an eco-conscious heart.

The John Wayne Gacys. Are they clowns? Are they serial killers? Are they liberal? Are they conservative? Are they all of the above?

The Architectural Tour Guide. Passionate about Chicago's storied buildings, they're a fountain of knowledge on every boat tour. Political stance? Structurally conservative, preserving the past with pride.

The Navy Pier Firework Fanatic. They never miss a summer fireworks display, finding magic in the night sky. Political leaning? Sparklingly bipartisan, with a love for shared spectacles.

The El Train Enthusiast. Mastering the city's public transit, they advocate for its efficiency and accessibility. Likely liberal, supporting public solutions for urban mobility.

The Blues Club Regular. Immersed in the soulful sounds of Chicago's historic blues scene, they live for live music. Political stance? Rhythmically liberal, with a deep appreciation for cultural roots.

The Grant Park Picnicker. With a blanket and a basket, they're a staple of the summer music festivals and outdoor cinema. Politically? Harmoniously liberal, savoring the city's communal spaces.

The Hot Dog Purist. No ketchup, ever. They uphold Chicago's hot dog traditions with religious fervor. Political leaning? Conservatively culinary, sticking to the tried-and-true.

The Polar Plunge Daredevil. Braving Lake Michigan's icy waters for charity, they're fearless in the face of frost. Political stance? Chillingly liberal, diving into social causes headfirst.

The Gold Coast Gentrifier. Dwelling in one of the city's most upscale areas, they walk the line between preservation and modernization. Likely conservative, valuing heritage and high property values.

The Street Art Seeker. They're on a constant quest for the city's most vibrant murals and graffiti, celebrating urban creativity. Politically? Progressively liberal, with a love for street-level expression.

The Harold's Chicken Shack Fanatic. Swearing by this Chicago institution, they know the secret to the perfect chicken is all in the sauce. Political leaning? Flavorfully independent, with a loyalty to local legends.

The Urban Gardener. Transforming rooftops and empty lots into green oases, they're sowing the seeds of sustainability. Political stance? Green, with a hands-in-the-dirt approach to change.

The Chicago History Museum Buff. Fascinated by the city's tumultuous past, from the Great Fire to the World's Fair, they're a walking encyclopedia. Likely conservative, with a reverence for history.

The Lincoln Park Zoo Advocate. Supporting conservation and education, they're passionate about the city's free zoo. Politically? Liberal, with a big heart for animal welfare.

The "It's Called The Sears Tower" Traditionalist. Refusing to call it Willis, they stand firm on the iconic skyscraper's original name. Political leaning? Nostalgically conservative, clinging to the classics.

How to Tell if Someone is Liberal or Conservative in Atlanta

The Peachtree Navigator. This individual knows every twist and turn of the Peachtree-named streets—yes, all 71 of them. Armed with an encyclopedic knowledge of Atlanta's most confusingly named roads, the Peachtree Navigator can guide you from Peachtree Heights to Peachtree Valley without breaking a sweat. They're often seen with a local brew in hand, explaining the difference between West Peachtree and Peachtree Battle Avenue to bewildered tourists. Political Leanings: Undefined. Their only allegiance is to the streets.

The Delta / CNN / Coca-Cola Junkies. This person came to Atlanta in the early 1990s, in what everyone thought was its heyday. They recall where they were on September 18, 1990 when the International Olympic Committee awarded

the 1996 Summer Olympics to Atlanta. 1990 - when the Atlanta metropolitan area had a mere 2,000,000 residents. This person dreams of Tom Glavine, Greg Maddux, and John Smoltz and once saw Ted Turner at the Buckhead Diner. Political Leanings: Well, Georgia used to be reliably red.

The BeltLine Bruncher. Weekend mornings find this species in their natural habitat: the bustling BeltLine, where they engage in the sacred ritual of brunch. Sporting athleisure with a mimosa in hand, the BeltLine Bruncher debates the merits of avocado toast versus chicken and waffles, all while planning their next stop at a nearby art installation or pop-up market. Political Leanings: Likely liberal, with a strong belief in the power of bottomless mimosas for social change.

The Biebs. This person is Justin Bieber.

The Hartsfield-Jackson Hustler. With a suitcase that's seen more miles than a '90s tour van, the Hartsfield-Jackson Hustler navigates the world's busiest airport with the ease of a seasoned pilot. They have the TSA PreCheck process down to a science and can recount the best dining spots across every concourse. This person can't stop talking about the fucking airport even when they're not at the airport and when no travel is imminent. Political Leanings: Conservative in their travel habits, liberal in their airport dining choices.

The Midtown Mixologist. This cocktail connoisseur is the lifeblood of Midtown's vibrant nightlife. They're not just serving drinks; they're curating experiences, one artisanal cocktail at a time. With a flair for the dramatic and a knack for infusing local flavors into every creation, the Midtown Mixologist is as much a part of Atlanta's culture as the skyline itself. Political Leanings: A mix of both, stirring up conversations and cocktails that blur the lines.

The I Miss Left Eye Lopez. This person knows exactly where they were on June 9, 1994 when TLC singer Lisa "Left Eye" Lopez set Falcons' wide receiver Andre Rison's house on fire. Political Leanings: Don't go chasin' waterfalls.

The Piedmont Park Picnicker. On any given sunny day, the Piedmont Park Picnicker can be found sprawled on a blanket, surrounded by a spread that's part gourmet, part Southern comfort. This person is a master of relaxation, turning a simple picnic into an art form, complete with a soundtrack of live music drifting over from the nearby park stage. Political Leanings: Apolitical, unless you challenge their choice of picnic spots.

The Georgia Aquarium Gazer. This serene soul finds tranquility in the depths of the Georgia Aquarium's oceanic wonders. They can spend hours marveling at the balletic movements of whale sharks and manta rays, often sparking conversations about marine conservation with anyone who'll listen. Political Leanings: Liberal, with a deep blue commitment to environmental preservation.

They're Called Boobs Ed. This person knew Julia Roberts when. Political Leanings: Liberal chic with a penchant for tradition.

The Give Tyler Perry An Oscar. This person thinks Tyler Perry was merely the next perfect hybrid of Marlon Brando, Steven Spielberg, and Sidney Poitier when he conceptualized, wrote, produced, directed, and starred in the Madea movies. Then he bought Fort McPherson and turned it into a film studio and ... seriously. Give Tyler Perry an Oscar already. Political Leanings: Dramatically liberal, with a penchant for progressive plots and diverse casts.

The Sweet Auburn Soul Foodie. A connoisseur of comfort food, this epicurean explorer is on a perpetual quest for Atlanta's best soul food. From collard greens to cornbread, they know where to find the most authentic and satisfying dishes, often reminiscing about the rich history of the Sweet Auburn neighborhood. Political Leanings: Deeply rooted in tradition with a generous seasoning of progressive ideals.

The Centennial Olympic Park Jogger. This fitness enthusiast uses the iconic Centennial Olympic Park as their personal track, jogging past the Fountain of Rings and the remnants of the 1996 Summer Olympics. They're all about personal bests and park aesthetics, often doubling as an informal tour guide for out-of-towners curious about Atlanta's Olympic legacy. Political Leanings: Runs the gamut but leans towards a competitive spirit in all arenas.

The ATL United Ultra. More than a fan, this individual lives and breathes Atlanta United soccer. Decked out in black, red, and gold, they lead chants, wave flags, and embody the spirit of the game with a passion that rivals any European football fanatic. Political Leanings: Uniting a diverse fan base, their politics are as inclusive as their love for the game.

The Tech Village Visionary. With a startup pitch at the ready, this tech-savvy entrepreneur is a fixture in Atlanta's thriving Tech Village. They're always networking, innovating, and dreaming up the next big thing in tech, all while championing the city as the Silicon Valley of the South. Political Leanings: Forward-thinking and generally liberal, with a firm belief in the power of technology to drive societal change.

The Emory. Esteemed academic or diligent student, the Emory Educator is steeped in the pursuit of knowledge. Whether debating politics over coffee in Decatur or leading groundbreaking research, they are a pillar of Atlanta's intellectual community. Political Leanings: Academically liberal, always advocating for evidence-based policies and open-minded discourse.

The High Museum Art Aficionado. This patron of the arts spends their weekends wandering the sleek halls of the High Museum, immersed in the latest exhibits. They have a keen eye for contemporary art and a deep appreciation for the museum's architecturally stunning environment. Political Leanings: Aesthetically liberal, believing in the transformative power of art to shape societal views.

The Dragon Con Cosplayer. Every year, this imaginative soul painstakingly crafts their costume for Atlanta's famed Dragon Con, becoming a living embodiment of their favorite character. They revel in the camaraderie of fandoms and the creative expression that the convention celebrates. Political Leanings: Fantastically apolitical, their allegiance lies with their chosen realm or galaxy.

The Piedmont Park Dog Walker. Equipped with an array of leashes and treats, this canine aficionado is a staple of Piedmont Park's lush landscapes. They navigate the dog parks and paths with a pack of pampered pooches, advocating for animal rights and green spaces with equal fervor. Political Leanings: A bipartisan love for pets, with a green thumb leaning for park conservation.

The Chattahoochee River Rafter. Seeking adventure in the city's natural wonders, this thrill-seeker tackles the rapids of the Chattahoochee River with gusto. They're all about the great outdoors, conservation, and the adrenaline rush of navigating Atlanta's waterways. Political Leanings: Fluid, with a current towards environmental stewardship and natural resource enjoyment.

The Mercedes-Benz Stadium Tailgater. Before every Falcons game, this superfan sets up camp in the shadow of the Mercedes-Benz Stadium, grill ablaze and team flags flying high. They're all about community, camaraderie, and the unifying power of football. Political Leanings: Team-spirited, where loyalty to the game transcends political divides.

How to Catch er uh I Mean Identify the One Liberal Person in Tulsa, Oklahoma

Go to Tulsa, Oklahoma.

Make a liberal's favorite sandwich. (That's arugula and "turkey" that is really tofu on bread that identifies as neither whole wheat nor rye but is definitely not white.)

Setup a lemonade stand somewhere in the arts district except cross out lemonade and instead write "Abortions 5 cents." You can still sell lemonade if you want so long as you use free range lemons.

Set up one of those cartoon traps where you set up a box with a stick and a storing tied to the stick. Like this:

Except instead of cheese put the non-binary sandwich under the box.

Wait. You won't have to wait long. The liberal will not be working obviously and will smell the aroma from the free handout and the bargain abortion wherever they are; assuming their Prius is charged. But if you're in a hurry to get back to work (someone has to) you can play Taylor Swift on your speakers.

When the liberal tires to grab the non-boinary sandwich, pull that string.

ou just caught er uh I mean identified the Tulsa liberal!

How to Tell if Someone is Liberal or Conservative in Minneapolis

The Skyway Scamp. Strolling above the city streets with a mischievous glint, the Skyway Scamp lives by the Replacements' credo, "Anywhere's better than here." Dodging the 9-to-5 crowd with the agility of a street dancer, they're the embodiment of urban freedom, turning the glass-encased bridges into their personal playground. Whether they're leaving cryptic lyrics from "Skyway" on coffee shop napkins while sittin' down and waitin' for a ride with unsuspecting commuters, their spirit is as infectious as the opening chords of a Tommy Stinson guitar. Politically: Crypto-fascist.

The Little Red Corvette Driver. In a city where the winters are harsh and the summers blaze, the Little Red Corvette Driver cruises down Hennepin Avenue, embodying the sleek, daring essence of Prince's classic. With the top down and "I guess I should've known by the way you parked your car sideways" blasting from the speakers, this character is all about making an entrance and leaving a trail of intrigue and admiration in their wake. Politically: Free-market Byzantism.

The Alex Chilton. The Alex Chilton is the unsung hero of the Minneapolis music scene. Haunting dive bars and underground venues, they champion the cause of "Children by the million" who sing along to songs yet to be recognized as anthems. Their heart beats to the rhythm of unsung melodies, and their mission is to ensure that no chord goes unstrummed and no chorus unsung. Politically: Orthodox Marxism.

The Raspberry Beret Eccentric. Walking in through the out door of every office building, Target, and thrift store in Uptown, the Raspberry Beret Eccentric is a vision of vintage flair and flamboyant charm. They mix and match eras with the ease of a DJ blending tracks, turning sidewalks into runways. Their mantra, "She wore a raspberry beret, the kind you find in a second-hand store," is a testament to their belief that style is about creativity, not labels. Politically: Conservative.

The Androgynous Anarchist. This enigmatic figure is as elusive as the northern lights, challenging norms and turning heads from the Warehouse District to Lyn-Lake. With an aura that's part mystique, part electric energy, they channel Prince's fearless individuality, leaving a wake of whispered questions: "Is that a man or a woman?" "Do they seek to abolish all institutions and replace the state with voluntary free associations or "Do they lean more anarcho-capitalist or more revolutionary-socialit?" In a city known for its openness, the Androgynous Anarchist is a living ode to the line, "I'm not a woman; I'm not a man; I am something that you'll never understand." Politically: Anarchist. But androgynously.

The Bastards of Young Rebel. In the heart of the city where the Mississippi roars, the Bastards of Young Rebel stands tall on the Stone Arch Bridge, a silhouette against the setting sun. Their anthem is the raw, unapologetic energy of The Replacements' "Bastards of Young." Disenchanted yet defiant, they rally against the ennui of the digital age, a vinyl record under one arm and a spray paint can in the other, ready to leave their mark on the city's canvas. Politically: Fully automated luxury communism.

The Darling Nikki Nostalgist. Usually found in the lobby of a luxury downtown hotel masturbating with a magazine, the Darling Nikki Nostalgist is usually just wasting time, their gaze lost in yearning to relive the glory days of the 1991 World Series[15]. They recount the highs and lows of the Minnesota Vikings[16],

---

15   The 1991 World Series is widely regarded as one of the most thrilling championships in Major League Baseball history, culminating in a dramatic victory for the Minnesota Twins over the Atlanta Braves. This 88th edition of the World Series was notable not just for the high stakes and intense competition, but also for the remarkable narratives surrounding both teams. The Twins and Braves had each finished the previous season at the bottom of their respective leagues, making their ascent to the championship round a historic feat in baseball annals. The series extended to seven games, with the outcome often hanging by a thread—five games were decided by a single run, four were won in the final at-bat, and three went into extra innings, showcasing the evenly matched and fiercely competitive nature of the two teams. The climax of the series came in the seventh game, a nail-biting showdown that remained scoreless through nine innings and ventured into the tenth. The Twins emerged victorious with a 1-0 win, thanks in large part to the heroics of pitcher Jack Morris, who delivered a 10-inning complete game shutout and earned MVP honors for his performance. The 1991 World Series not only celebrated the Twins' championship victory but also stood as a testament to the unpredictability and excitement of baseball, capturing the imagination of fans and earning a special place in the sport's history.

16   Being a Minnesota Vikings fan is akin to enduring a roller coaster of highs and lows, marked by moments of near triumph and sudden disappointment. Since their inception in 1961, the Vikings have yet to secure a Super Bowl victory, despite several close calls and moments of brilliance. Memorable disappointments include Gary Anderson's missed field goal in the 1998 playoffs after a stellar season, the crushing 41-0 defeat to the Giants in the 2000 NFC Championships, and Brett Favre's costly interception in the 2010 NFC Championship game against the Saints. The infamous Herschel Walker trade in 1989 is often cited as one of the worst deals in NFL history, contributing to the team's struggles. Despite these

along with tales of legendary gigs and chance encounters with Jimmy Jam and Terry Lewis. Politically: Merciless Monarchist.

The Unsatisfied Urbanite. Leaning against the graffiti-adorned walls of the 7th St. Entry, the Unsatisfied Urbanite embodies the restless spirit of Minneapolis. They're the voice of a generation caught between nostalgia and the relentless pace of change, finding solace in the strum of a guitar and the honesty of lyrics that ask, "Look me in the eye, then tell me that I'm satisfied." Politically: Enlightened absolutism.

The Purple Rain Prophet. When the summer storms roll in, painting the skies in dramatic hues, the Purple Rain Prophet takes to the rooftops, arms outstretched, welcoming the deluge. They find a sacred connection in the rain, a cleansing, renewing force that binds the city together under a canopy of water and song. Politcally: Violet Vanguardism.

The Can't Hardly Wait Dreamer. Perched on the edge of the Mississippi, gazing at the twinkling lights of the city, the Can't Hardly Wait Dreamer lives in a perpetual state of anticipation, their heart a ticking clock synced to the rhythm of The Replacements' "Can't Hardly Wait" and the theme song from the Mary Tyler Moore Show. They're the embodiment of youthful longing and the eternal belief that something, somewhere, is about to change their world forever. Politically: Oligarchical Plutocacy.

The Take Me With U Tourist. This wide-eyed wanderer, with a map in one hand and a camera in the other, explores the city's landmarks. They start early at the Chain of Lakes, usually begin with a bike rental at Lake Calhoun and enjoy its vibrant beach and watersports scene before pedaling east to picturesque Lake of the Isles, perfect for a leisurely stroll or a kayak adventure. They continue to Lake Harriet, where they can unwind at the bandshell with live music or explore the rose garden. They finish at serene Cedar Lake, ideal

---

setbacks, the Vikings have had their moments of glory, such as the "Minneapolis Miracle" in 2018, where Stefon Diggs scored a last-second touchdown against the Saints, and the record-breaking comeback against the Colts in 2022. Adrian Peterson's single-game rushing record in 2007 and Randy Moss's dominant performance against the Cowboys in 1998 stand out as individual achievements. Currently, Justin Jefferson is making waves, setting records for receiving yards in his first three seasons. These moments of success offer hope to Vikings fans, who continue to dream of a Super Bowl victory despite the team's tumultuous history.

for a quiet picnic or a dip in its hidden beach, all the while utilizing the city's well-connected bike paths and don't forget to stop at local cafés and eateries along the way for refreshments. They seek not just sights, but experiences, hoping to be whisked away on an adventure that mirrors Minneapolis's natural world of imagination and wonder. Politically: Muscular Liberalism.

The Kiss Connoisseur. A fixture in the chicest clubs of the Warehouse District, the Kiss Connoisseur is a master of allure, drawing admirers with a magnetism as potent as the opening riff of Prince's "Kiss." Their philosophy? Life's too short for subtlety, and a little bit of mystery goes a long way. In a city known for its chill, they bring the heat, one smoldering kiss at a time. Politically: Conservative.

The Here Comes A Regular Regular. At the heart of every neighborhood bar, there's a stool that might as well have their name on it. The Here Comes A Regular Regular works up a mean, mean thirst, heads to a bar, and offers up wisdom and witticisms with the ease of a practiced barstool bard. They are poignant reminder of the beauty found in everyday connections and the solace of a familiar face in a crowded room. Politically: Neo-Corporate Welfarism.

The I Could Never Take The Place Of Your Man Adventurer. With a spirit as free as the chorus of Prince's vibrant tune, this Minneapolitan is a whirlwind of charisma and charm, never staying long enough to break hearts, but always leaving a lasting impression. They're the quintessential summer fling, a story to be told with a wistful smile, embodying the fleeting, ephemeral joy of a Minneapolis summer. Politically: Christuian Egalitarianist.

The I Will Dare Devil. Despite their name, this person rarely ventures outside of the Mall of America, which offers an unparalleled array of activities that go far beyond traditional shopping experiences. The I Will Dare Devil loves how the Mall of America elevates shopping to an extraordinary experience, with over 500 stores and a diverse array of more than 50 dining options to cater to every taste and preference. Fashion aficionados find a paradise in the vast selection of boutiques and flagship stores ranging from high-end designers like Michael Kors and Coach to popular brands such as Zara and H&M. Tech enthusiasts explore the latest gadgets and innovations at the Apple Store and Best Buy, while beauty lovers can indulge in a plethora of choices from

Sephora to Lush Cosmetics. The mall is a haven for unique finds too, with specialty shops like the LEGO Store and the M&M's World adding a fun twist to shopping. Politically: Conservative.

The When Doves Cry Poet. In a world that's so cold, the When Dove Cries Poet just yearns for the quiet corners of coffee shops and the dimly lit recesses of poetry slams so they can channel their raw emotion into poetry. Their verses explore the complexities of love and loss, the nuances of human emotion, against the backdrop of a city that's as multifaceted as their poetry. Politically: Ecoauthoritanism.

The Let's Go Crazy Life Coach. Are these people ever going to let the elevator bring them down? No. Politically: Radical Centrist.

The Swingin' Party Socialite. The life of every gathering, this character brings The Replacements' "Swingin' Party" to life, hosting soirees that are the stuff of local legend. Their abode is a mosaic of Minneapolis culture, where artists, musicians, and dreamers converge, finding common ground in the eclectic beats of the city's heart. Politically: Neo-Republicanism.

The Diamonds and Pearls Dazzler. Adorned in diamonds and pearls this dazzler sees the world through a lens of opulence and fantasy, turning the streets of Minneapolis into a stage for their lavish daydreams. They're a walking testament to the power of belief and the beauty of aspirations, no matter how grand. Politically: Venezuelan Whig.

The Waitress In The Sky. Navigating the city with the grace of an in-flight professional, this character brings hospitality down to earth but also brings hospitality to the stars, serving up kindness and care with the efficiency of a seasoned pro. They're a reminder that, in the hustle and bustle of city life, a little courtesy goes a long way. Politically: New Deal Liberal.

How to Convert er uh I mean Identify the One Conservative Person in Portland, Oregon

First, drive around the city in a Dodge Charger General Lee replica. Blast Lee Greenwood's "God Bless the U.S.A." This won't necessarily help you identify the conservative - they're in the office working - but it will annoy the liberals. And watching them run for cover will be fun.

But to identify the one conservative person in Portland, you'll need a plan. It starts with a hologram of Ronald Reagan. Get a hologram machine that can make a Ronald Regan hologram. Then get a horse. Then wait until 5:00 p.m. when the downtown offices clear out. But the conservative won't be in that crowd. The conservative will be working late because they need to make more money because taxes. Be sure to feed the horse because the conservative will be working late. Also make sure the hologram machine is adequately charged or has new batteries. How do hologram machines run? Are they electric? If so, you'll need to be near an outlet.

Anyway, it'll be approaching 9:00 p.m. The conservative will still be working to make extra money because taxes, turn on the Ronald Reagan hologram machine, get on your horse, and make the Ronald Regan hologram say "Mr. Gorbachev - tear down this wall!" and the conservative will come see it.

How to Tell if Someone is Liberal or Conservative in Houston

The Space City Stargazer. This amateur astronomer takes the "Space City" moniker to heart, setting up telescopes in unexpected urban locales to share cosmic views with passersby. They claim to have discovered a new constellation shaped like Texas.

The Bayou Biker Bard. Roaming the bayous on a bike adorned with poetic verses, this bard stops at every bridge to recite tales of Houston's history and heart, blending local lore with lyrical flights of fancy. Political Leanings: Lyrically liberal, pedaling verses of social justice and environmental stewardship.

The Rodeo Drive-In Dandy. Decked out in rhinestone-studded cowboy boots and a ten-gallon hat, this urban cowboy brings rodeo flair to Houston's drive-in theaters, turning tailgating into a Texas-sized spectacle. Political Leanings: Cinematically conservative, with a penchant for Westerns and traditional values.

The Art Car Artisan. Creator of the most outlandish vehicle in the annual Art Car Parade, their car is half sculpture, half machine, and completely Houston. They champion the city's eclectic art scene with every mile driven. Political Leanings: Creatively communal, driving forward the agenda of public art for all.

The Medical Center Mystic. Believing in the healing power of both science and spirits, this healthcare worker by day becomes a holistic healer by night, blending medical knowledge with ancient remedies in the shadows of Houston's medical skyscrapers.

The Galleria Glider. An ice-skating enthusiast who believes the rink at the Galleria is a portal to another dimension. They're seen performing elaborate routines, convinced each spin and jump brings them closer to uncovering a cosmic secret. Political Leanings: Dimensionally democratic, advocating for alternate realities and universal healthcare.

The Tex-Mex Chef Shaman. In their kitchen-laboratory, this culinary wizard concocts dishes that are part feast, part ritual, infusing classic Tex-Mex with exotic herbs and whispered incantations, promising enlightenment with every bite. Political Leanings: Gastronomically green, with a manifesto for sustainable agriculture and enchanted eating.

The Hermann Park Hermit. Shrouded in mystery, this character claims to be the guardian of the park's secrets, communicating with the statues and the ducks in a language only they understand, offering breadcrumbs of wisdom to those who listen.

The Enron Antihero. Beneath this person's façade of success lies a web of deceit. Like their namesake, this person's financial practices are characterized by the use of special purpose entities and dubious accounting methods. They obscured massive debts and they inflate profits! Eventually, their façade will crumble when analyst questions and a subsequent SEC investigation unveil the extent of their financial manipulation. Political Leanings: Anti-Sarbanes, Anti-Oxley.

The Heights Hipster Historian. This retro-revivalist roams the Heights, documenting its transformation from suburban outpost to urban cool, all while campaigning for the preservation of its vintage charm in the face of modern development. Political Leanings: Nostalgically neutral, with a passion for the past that transcends party lines.

The Alley Theatre Phantom. A ghostly presence rumored to haunt the Alley Theatre, providing unsolicited critiques to performers and occasionally inspiring playwrights with whispers of forgotten dramas and spectral insights. Political Leanings: Dramatically deceased, their only caucus is with the muses of the past.

The Discovery Green Druid. This urban druid believes the park is built on a ley line and conducts rituals to keep the city's energy in balance, blending eco-activism with ancient rites beneath the shadow of downtown skyscrapers. Political Leanings: Green in every sense, advocating for urban green spaces as spiritual and environmental renewal sanctuaries.

The Lone Star Librarian. Guardian of a hidden library that houses the true tales of Texas, this keeper of stories rides through the city on horseback, sharing tales of heroism and heartbreak that weave the fabric of Houston's identity. Political Leanings: Literarily libertarian, believing in the freedom of stories to shape society.

The Buffalo Bayou Buccaneer. This modern-day pirate plies the waters of Buffalo Bayou in a solar-powered skiff, searching for hidden treasures and cleaning up the waterways with a crew of environmentally-minded misfits. Political Leanings: Pirate-partisan, with a code that values clean waters and community above all.

The Westheimer Wizard. Master of illusions, this street magician uses the bustling backdrop of Westheimer Road to perform acts that blur the line between reality and magic, drawing crowds and skeptics alike into their mysterious world. Political Leanings: Magically moderate, their only allegiance is to the awe and wonder of their audience.

The Astrodome Oracle. Dwelling in the shadows of the abandoned Astrodome, this soothsayer claims the structure is a giant crystal ball, offering visions of Houston's future to those brave enough to venture into its echoing depths. Political Leanings: Futuristically nostalgic, caught between the glory of past spectacles and visions of renewal.

The Kemah Boardwalk Buccaneer. A rogue with a heart of gold, this character captains a carousel at the Kemah Boardwalk, spinning tales of high-seas adventures and pirate lore to the delight of children and the amusement of adults. Political Leanings: Swashbuckling socialist, sharing the booty of joy and laughter in equal measure.

The Rice University Riddler. This academic enigma poses perplexing puzzles and riddles around campus, challenging the minds of students and faculty alike, believing that the key to enlightenment lies in the journey, not the answer.

Tom

Suzanne Vega's "Tom's Diner" presents a vivid narrative set in the everyday locale of a diner, with Tom, the owner, at its heart. Through the song's observational lyrics and the monochrome rhythm of city life it paints, one can conclude that Tom is a centrist. He embodies a balanced approach to life and business.

Tom's diner, described in Vega's meticulous and almost journalistic detail, becomes a microcosm of urban life, where various facets of society converge over coffee. Tom's role as the steward of this communal space suggests a centrist's appreciation for the middle ground, where differing views and lives intersect harmoniously. The song's portrayal of mundane, yet intimate moments, like the woman "shaking her umbrella" or the "bells of the cathedral," reflects a centrist perspective that finds value in stability and the quiet continuity of daily life. Tom's ability to maintain this neutral ground, welcoming to all, mirrors a centrist's skill in navigating diverse viewpoints and fostering a sense of community without veering too far into any one ideological extreme.

Furthermore, the diner's role as a haven from the complexities of the outside world, where simple pleasures and human connections take precedence, speaks to a centrist ideal of practicality and relatability, grounded in the real and the tangible.

The Tom of "Tom's Diner" emerges as a figure embodying centrism, his diner a metaphor for the balance and moderation that define his approach to life, business, and the diverse tapestry of the urban experience.

Alison

Elvis Costello's "Alison" is a haunting ballad that weaves a complex tapestry of emotions, hinting at unrequited love and deep-seated regret. Through the song's poignant lyrics and melancholic melody, Alison emerges as a figure embodying conservative values, particularly in the realms of love, loss, and the sanctity of past relationships.

The line, "Sometimes I wish that I could stop you from talking when I hear the silly things that you say," suggests a longing for preservation and a desire to maintain an idealized image of Alison, reflecting a conservative inclination to hold onto the past and resist change that could tarnish cherished memories. And also like how no one listens to women like Anita Hill and Christine Blasey Ford when they hear the silly things that Anita Hill and Christine Blasey Ford say. And Alison is ok with this? Why not just call this song Lisa Murkowski or Susan Collins. Or Susan Murkowski. Why not?

Moreover, the song's refrain, "My aim is true," speaks to a commitment and fidelity that conservative perspectives on relationships frequently emphasize. The narrator's devotion, despite Alison's apparent indifference or unawareness, highlights a traditional view of love as enduring and unyielding, even in the face of unreciprocated feelings.

Costello's portrayal of Alison, coupled with the narrator's introspective and somber reflection on their connection, underscores a yearning for what once was—a quintessentially conservative sentiment that values the depth and permanence of emotional bonds, even when they lead to personal heartache.

Through "Alison," Costello crafts a narrative steeped in conservative notions of love's lasting impact, the pain of letting go, the importance of keeping a woman silent, and the poignant beauty of holding onto the idealized remnants of a relationship long after it has faded from reality.

What to Do If Stuck in a Barrel Going Over Niagara Falls with a Conservative

Congratulations! You've found yourself in a classic pickle, stuffed into a barrel with a conservative on a one-way trip over Niagara Falls. Fear not! Here's your foolproof guide to handle this tumbling conundrum with flair and a hint of bipartisan spirit.

1. Check Your Barrel-mates' Beliefs at the Door. As you squeeze in, remember to leave little room for political debate. There's no space for tax reform discussions when you're compacted tighter than a conservative's wallet during tax season.

2. Stockpile Your Supplies. In the likely case that your barrel buddy has packed nothing but copies of the Constitution and an Ayn Rand novel for sustenance, make sure to bring some snacks. Energy bars might just replace trickle-down economics as your favorite kind of "bar."

3. Initiate Small Talk. Start with safe topics like the weather (specifically the mist from the falls which is about to soak you). Avoid triggering topics like the environment, unless you want to debate climate change while actually submerged in water.

4. Practice Your Smile. You'll want to look good for the inevitable photo op, even as you plunge to watery depths. Perfect your grip-and-grin, because, let's face it, this might be your last chance to impress voters— or at least fish.

5. Plan Your Escape. As you approach the drop, it might be a good time to reflect on your life choices. But, more importantly, on how fast you can swim. Remember, conservative or not, you'll both need to paddle like the economy depends on it!

So, there you have it! Just remember, when going over the falls in a barrel, it's less about the political lean and more about the physical lean—lean in and brace yourself!

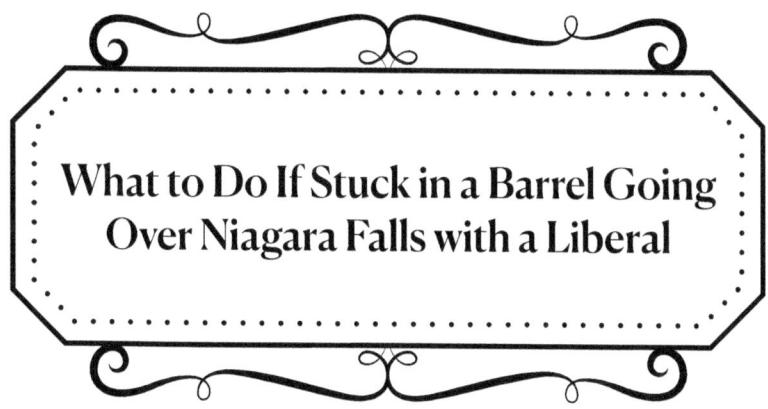

What to Do If Stuck in a Barrel Going Over Niagara Falls with a Liberal

So, you're about to experience the literal waterfall of progressive ideas by heading over Niagara Falls in a barrel with a liberal. No worries! Here's how to make the most of your splashy journey without capsizing the ideological boat.

1. Embrace the Metaphor. Just as you embrace the free fall, embrace the metaphorical implications of going over the falls with a liberal. It's all about progress, right? Even if it's straight down.

2. Pack Your Emotional Support Items. Since your liberal companion may have brought an assortment of protest signs, reusable straws, and a playlist of NPR podcasts, be sure to bring items that comfort you. Perhaps a nice, soothing tea to calm both your nerves and any heated debates.

3. Keep the Conversation Fluid. Discuss fluid dynamics as a way to cleverly dodge more contentious topics. If that fails, there's always discussing actual water—the non-partisan kind surrounding your barrel.

4. Sustainability Matters. Compliment their choice of a barrel. After all, it's eco-friendlier than a gas-guzzling boat, right? Bonus points if the barrel is upcycled or made from sustainably sourced materials.

5. Prepare for the Impact. As you near the fall, remember to plan your exit strategy. Liberals are great at grassroots organizing, so they might just have a community-supported rescue team on standby.

6. Document the Experience. If your barrel mate hasn't already started a live tweet session or a TikTok live stream, now might be a good time to start. After all, if you're going to take the plunge, why not go viral doing it?

There you have it—your guide to surviving Niagara Falls in a barrel with a liberal. Remember, it's all about enjoying the ride, or at least, finding common ground somewhere between the riverbed and the ideological divide!

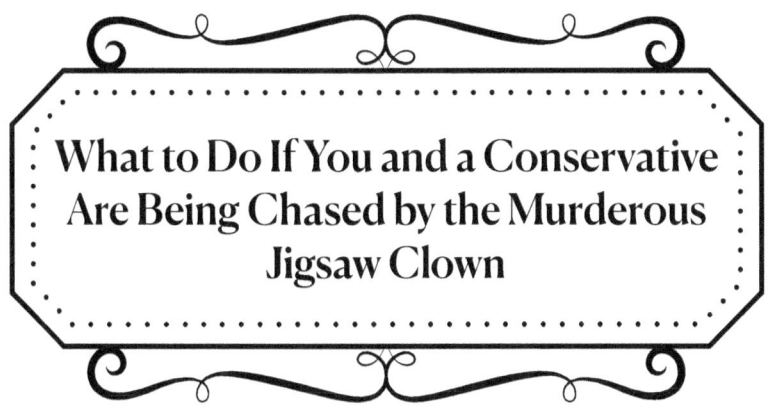

What to Do If You and a Conservative Are Being Chased by the Murderous Jigsaw Clown

If you find yourself in the unnerving predicament of being chased by the infamous Jigsaw clown, alongside a conservative, fear not! Here's how to navigate this harrowing horror scenario with a conservative twist.

1. Stick to Conservative Spaces. Start by running to the nearest bank or multinational corporation. Jigsaw's penchant for ironic punishment might make these places of fiscal sanctuary less appealing targets.

2. Argue the Cost-Benefit Analysis. As you dash for safety, use the time to discuss with your conservative companion the economic implications of being in a horror movie. How much does fear cost, anyway? This might distract them from the existential dread and keep their mind on fiscal matters.

3. Quote the Constitution. If Jigsaw corners you, have your conservative friend start quoting the Second Amendment. It might not stop a clown with a penchant for puzzles, but it will at least give you a moment to think of a real plan.

4. Propose a Free Market Solution. Suggest to Jigsaw that instead of chasing you, he should consider monetizing his puzzle-based terror. A subscription model, perhaps? Your conservative companion will nod appreciatively at this entrepreneurial spirit.

5. Rely on Traditional Values. In a clutch moment, remind your conservative partner about the importance of individual responsibility—especially their responsibility to help you get out of this mess alive.

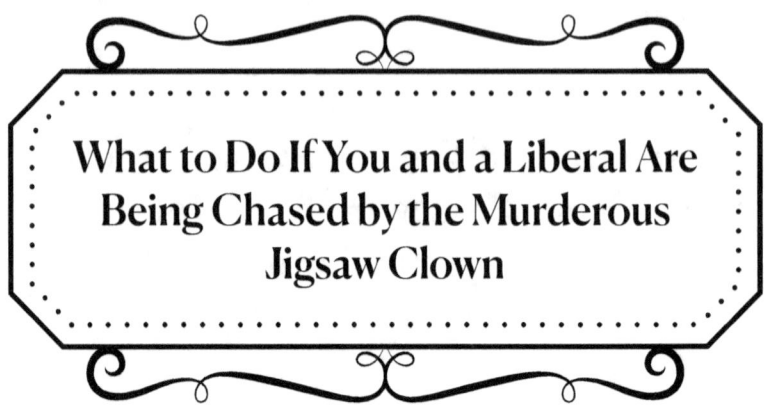

What to Do If You and a Liberal Are Being Chased by the Murderous Jigsaw Clown

Caught in a chase with the menacing Jigsaw clown and a liberal by your side? Here's how to handle this thriller with a liberal approach.

1. Seek a Safe Space. Immediately seek out the nearest community center or organic coffee shop. These liberal havens might offer the perfect hiding spots, and Jigsaw could surely use a fair-trade coffee break.

2. Debate Social Justice. Use the opportunity to discuss with Jigsaw the social injustices of his actions. Perhaps your liberal companion can engage him in a debate about the ethics of his methods. This could buy you some precious time or, at the very least, confuse him.

3. Emphasize Rehabilitation Over Punishment. Convince Jigsaw to consider the rehabilitative approach rather than punitive. Suggest a workshop or a seminar. It might not stop him, but advocacy for reform is worth a shot.

4. Sustainable Escape Plans. Make sure any escape plan is environmentally friendly. Ditch the gas-guzzling cars for electric vehicles or bicycles. Your liberal companion will appreciate the effort to maintain a low carbon footprint during the escape.

5. Record Everything. Ensure your liberal friend is documenting the entire ordeal for a documentary that could be used to raise awareness about the psychological impacts of being chased by a murderous clown. Plus, if you survive, think of the film festival potential!

Navigating a horror scenario with either a conservative or liberal can add an interesting layer to your survival strategy. Whether it's through the lens of economic pragmatism or social justice, there's always a way to bring a bit of ideological flair to even the most dire situations!

What to Do If You and a Conservative Are in a Revenant Situation and There's Only Room for One of You in the Horse Carcass

Imagine the chilly predicament where you and a conservative must decide who gets the cozy confines of a horse carcass to survive a bitter cold night. Here's your practical guide to navigating this Revenant-style dilemma.

1. Economic Arguments: Start by suggesting a free-market approach. Propose an auction for the spot in the horse carcass. It's all about supply and demand, right? The highest bidder wins the warmth!

2. Founding Fathers' Quotes: While debating your fate, throw in some quotes from the Founding Fathers about survival and liberty. Maybe they didn't speak directly about horse carcass real estate, but you can get creative.

3. Deregulate the Horse: Argue that the horse carcass is over-regulated real estate and that free enterprise dictates that whoever can utilize the resource most efficiently should claim it. Efficiency here is measured in body heat retention, of course.

4. Investment Opportunities: Convince them that letting you in the carcass is an investment in future conservative policies. After all, you promise to advocate for lower taxes if you survive this frosty night.

5. Survival of the Fittest: When all else fails, revert to good old survivalist rhetoric. Maybe throw in a Teddy Roosevelt quote for good measure and wrestle for the spot—may the best free marketeer win!

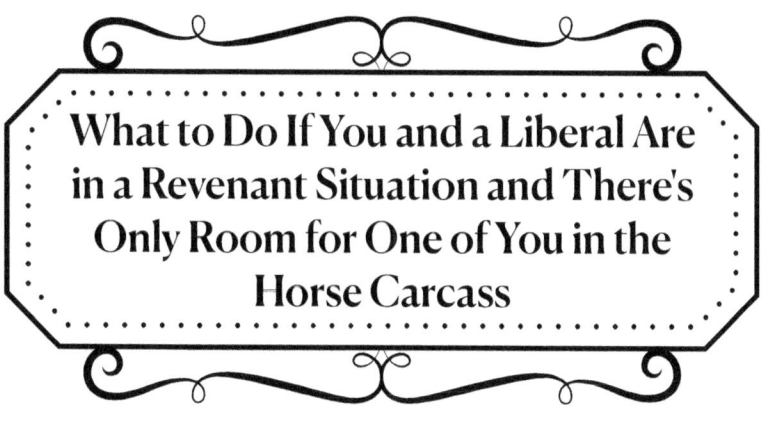

What to Do If You and a Liberal Are in a Revenant Situation and There's Only Room for One of You in the Horse Carcass

Caught in a freezing scenario with only one horse carcass and a liberal? Time to get craftily compassionate with your survival tactics.

1. Share the Wealth: Propose a time-share system for the carcass. You each get 20-minute intervals inside the carcass. It's only fair, right? Rotate to maintain equality and warmth.

2. Social Justice: Discuss the ethical implications of carcass hoarding. Maybe it's time the carcass was considered a communal good, to be shared by all—or at least by the both of you.

3. Green Alternatives: Suggest finding a more sustainable way to keep warm. Perhaps running in place or huddling next to a tree? It's all about reducing your carbon footprint, even in survival situations.

4. Documentary Evidence: Encourage them to think of the future documentary that could be made about this ordeal. The horse carcass dilemma: a tale of survival and sharing. The audience will love it!

5. Therapeutic Resolution: Initiate a deep, meaningful conversation about your feelings regarding the situation. Sometimes, a good heart-to-heart can warm you up more than a horse carcass ever could.

Navigating survival with either a conservative or liberal can be an absurdly humorous ordeal. Whether you choose the route of economic debate, social justice, or plain old survival tactics, remember—it's not just about staying alive, but how democratically you can share or monopolize that horse carcass!

What to Do If You and a Conservative Are Being Stalked by the Zodiac Killer

Caught in the chilling scenario of being stalked by the infamous Zodiac Killer with a conservative companion? Here's your survival guide to handle this threat with a right-leaning twist.

1. Constitutional Rights: Remind your conservative friend of their staunch support for the Second Amendment. This might be the moment to argue that personal defense is exactly why the Founding Fathers included it. Ready, aim, theorize!

2. Fiscal Responsibility: Suggest setting a budget for your survival resources. After all, fiscal conservatism doesn't have to stop just because you're being chased by a serial killer. Can you get a bulk discount on survival gear?

3. Deregulate Your Strategy: Propose that in situations as dire as this, the less government interference, the better. This means creating your own rules for evading the Zodiac. Free market survivalism, if you will.

4. Blame the Media: When all else fails, and if you're at a loss for what to do, take a moment to blame the media for sensationalizing the Zodiac Killer. It might not stop him, but at least it's a distraction.

5. Call for Backup: If things get too tense, remind your companion that it's perfectly conservative to ask for help—specifically from private security forces. Outsourcing isn't just for businesses, after all.

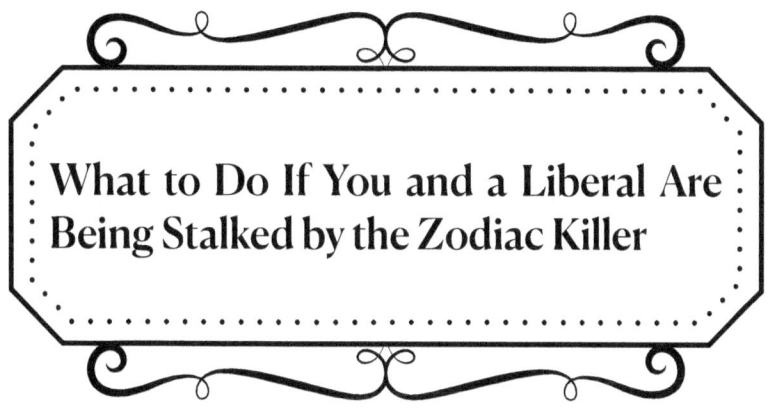

What to Do If You and a Liberal Are Being Stalked by the Zodiac Killer

If you find yourself in the precarious position of being hunted by the Zodiac Killer while accompanied by a liberal, here's how you might keep both of you alive.

1. Peaceful Negotiation: Encourage your liberal friend to consider the power of dialogue. Perhaps the Zodiac just needs to express himself in a less harmful way? Initiate a mediated conversation via safe distance.

2. Social Programs: Quickly devise a rehabilitation program for serial killers. Discuss how society has failed the Zodiac and brainstorm community-based solutions that could appeal to his better nature.

3. Environmental Hiding: Suggest hiding in an eco-friendly location. Maybe the local organic farm has a compost heap you can both hide in. It's sustainable and potentially very effective!

4. Raise Awareness: Turn this terrifying experience into a campaign about the dangers of glorifying serial killers in media. Live-tweet your evasion tactics to spread awareness (and maybe get some help).

5. Call for Collective Action: Nothing says "liberal" like organizing a group. If you can, mobilize a community action group to peacefully protest the Zodiac's actions. Strength in numbers might just save you.

Whether you're leveraging rights and responsibilities or advocating for peace and rehabilitation, make sure your approach is as strategic as it is satirical!

What to Do If You're in a Matt Damon Stuck on Mars Martian Situation with a Conservative

Stranded on Mars with a conservative? Here's how to make the best of your interplanetary predicament, leveraging some good old-fashioned right-wing ingenuity.

1. Emphasize Self-Reliance: Remind your conservative companion about the virtue of self-reliance. Together, channel your inner pioneers and set out to conquer the red planet with rugged individualism. Maybe start by claiming Mars as a tax-free zone.

2. Maximize Resources: Discuss the importance of free-market principles, even on Mars. Efficiently use your limited resources and maybe even set up a bartering system. Who knows? You could establish the first Martian economy.

3. Property Rights: Suggest dividing the habitat into private properties. This could motivate your companion to maintain and develop their space, stimulating a healthy dose of competition for who can grow the best space potatoes.

4. Conservative Space Policy: While waiting for rescue, plan the first conservative space policy for when humanity colonizes Mars. Topics could include governance, economic policies, and, naturally, space defense.

5. Traditional Values: Keep morale high by reminiscing about traditional values and how they can be applied on Mars. Perhaps Sunday roasts with whatever Martian equivalent you can muster up from your limited rations.

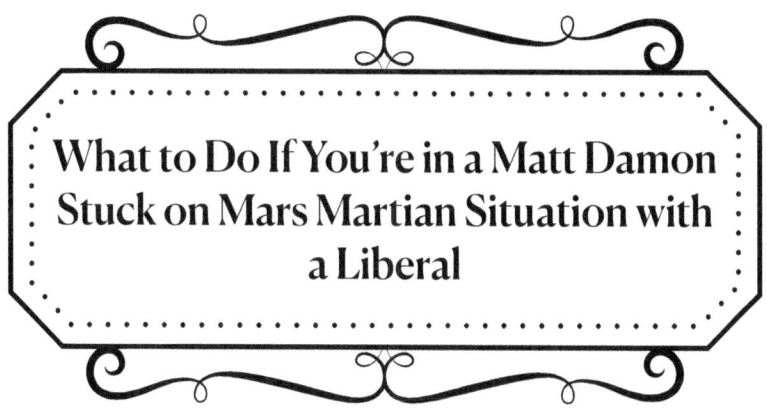

What to Do If You're in a Matt Damon Stuck on Mars Martian Situation with a Liberal

Stuck on Mars with a liberal? Here's how to survive the red planet by harnessing progressive energy and creativity.

1. Collective Resource Management: Immediately start managing your resources collectively. Emphasize the importance of shared responsibilities and equal distribution to maintain both your survival and democratic ideals.

2. Sustainable Living: Focus on sustainable living practices. Experiment with Martian soil to grow crops, and consider every way you can recycle and reuse materials. Your habitat should become a model green community.

3. Social Justice for Martians: Engage in discussions about the future rights of Martians and other potential life forms. It's never too early to plan for interplanetary social justice.

4. Inclusive Community Planning: While devising survival strategies, make sure all ideas are heard and valued. Your liberal companion will appreciate an inclusive approach, which could lead to innovative survival tactics.

5. Cultural Activities: Keep spirits high by organizing cultural activities. Maybe start a Martian film festival using whatever media you've brought, or hold debate nights to discuss Earth politics and dream about future Martian governance.

Surviving on Mars with a conservative or a liberal can turn into an enlightening experiment in small-scale societal building. Whether you're leveraging individualism or fostering community collaboration, each day can be a step toward thriving on a new world with a touch of familiar ideological flavor.

In the Kitchen with Ethel, Ethel Kennedy's "Almost Tuna" Salad

Welcome, dear friends, Today, we embark on a gastronomic journey to make my famous "Almost Tuna Salad." Why "almost," you ask? Let's dive in.

Ingredients:

- 2 cans of premium or low-grade tuna

- 1 stalk of celery, finely chopped

- 2 tablespoons of mayonnaise

- A sprinkle of optimism

- Parsley

Instructions:

1. Open the Cans of Tuna:

Begin with two cans of the finest tuna you can find. Or the most suitable tuna you can find. It won't matter. Open those tuna cans up and take a small taste of the first one to ensure quality—this is crucial. Then taste the second one - also crucial.

2. Continue Sampling:

Continue "sampling" the tuna for freshness. It's important to be thorough, so keep tasting. Use a spoon or a spatula or use a spoon and a spatula. I don't give a fuck. I just love tuna. Before you know it, you might find that the can starts to look shockingly empty. But fear not—this is all part of the process.

3. Improvise:

Soon the tuna will be all gone. Upon realizing there will not be enough tuna left for the actual salad, gracefully pivot to Plan B. Look at your finely chopped celery with pride as you declare it the new protagonist of your dish. If you get the celery from the garden out behind the main house, be sure to wash it really well as the Lawfords have a tendence to pee in the garden when they don't feel like wahsing their feet to go in the main house. How do I know this? Trust me. I know.

4. Mix What's Left:

Combine the lonely celery with a generous helping of mayonnaise. Mix well, as you recount the almost-heroic journey of the tuna that almost made it into the salad.

5. Serve.

Put a large sprig of parsley in your teeth to distract the guests when you serve them this. Plate your creation with a flourish and serve to your guests. As they take in the minimalist dish, a dish where the tuna is there in spirit and legend, if not in substance.

There you have it, a delightful salad with all the makings of a meal, minus the main ingredient, served with a side of laughter and a good story. Bon appétit!

Ethel Kennedy's "Tuna" Noodle Casserole Recipe

Let's step into Ethel's kitchen and watch the magic (or missteps) unfold.

Ingredients:

-2 cans of the best tuna

- 8 oz of egg noodles

- 1 cup of frozen peas

- 1 can of cream of mushroom soup

- 1 cup of shredded cheddar cheese

- 1 cup of crushed potato chips (for that crunch you won't find in the missing tuna)

- A generous pinch of diversion

Instructions:

1. Preheat Oven:

Begin by preheating your oven to 375 degrees.

2. Open those Cans of Tuna:

Open your cans of tuna. Take a small taste to ensure it's fit for your guests. It's only proper etiquette, after all.

3. The "Extended" Taste Test:

Continue tasting. It's important to be absolutely sure of the quality of that tuna—bite by bite, forkful by forkful. Just to cover your ass in case one of Eunice's kids is listening, loudly exclaim, "Oh dear, where did all the tuna go?"

4. Boil Noodles:

As the realization sets in that the tuna has vanished, boil your noodles as planned. They'll never know what hit them—or didn't. You could call over to the Shrivers to see if they have any tuna but then it becomes a whole thing. You know how Eunice's kids can be about the tuna.

5. Assemble the "Tuna-Free" Casserole:

In a state of mild panic mixed with a dash of creativity, mix the cooked noodles, peas, cream of mushroom soup, and half the cheese. Stir in the essence of the tuna.

6. Top and Bake:

Pour the mixture into a baking dish. Sprinkle the remaining cheese and crushed potato chips on top for that delightful crunch. Bake for 25 minutes, or until golden and bubbly, much like your story about how the tuna was there a minute ago.

7. Serve:

Serve your "Tuna" Noodle Casserole hot. As your guests dive into the surprisingly tuna-less dish, entertain them with the epic saga of how the tuna might have made it into the casserole, but made a delicious detour into history instead.

Bon appétit, or as we say in the Kennedy household, "What tuna?"

Ethel Kennedy's "Tuna" Croquettes Recipe

Step into the whimsical world of Ethel Kennedy's kitchen with her renowned "Tuna" Croquettes—where the tuna is more of a fleeting memory than an ingredient. Here's how you can recreate this elusive dish:

Ingredients:

- 2 cans of tuna

- 2 cups mashed potatoes

- 1 small onion, finely chopped

- 2 cloves garlic, minced

- 1/4 cup fresh parsley, chopped

- 1 egg, beaten

- 1 cup breadcrumbs

- Salt and pepper to taste

- Oil for frying

- A sense of adventure

Instructions:

1. Prepare Ingredients:

Warm up by chopping your onions and garlic, and prepare your mashed potatoes. The kitchen fills with the comforting aroma of home cooking and impending culinary creativity.

2. Open. Those. Big. Ass. Fucking. Cans. Of. Tuna.:

Open your fucking tuna cans with every intention of mixing it into your croquette batter. Tell the tuna that you are its destiny. Taste to confirm tuna quality—continue "confirming" until, quite inadvertently and quite by accident, you find yourself staring into an empty can.

3. Pivot Gracefully:

With the tuna tragically depleted, boldly embrace the potato. Add your onion, garlic, parsley, and a good seasoning of salt and pepper to the mashed potatoes. Who said anything about needing tuna for tuna croquettes?

4. Form those Goddamn Croquettes:

Shape the potato mixture into lovely, rounded croquettes. Dip those motherfuckers into the beaten egg, then gently roll them in breadcrumbs. Or roll them not gently, it don't matter.

5. Fry to Perfection:

Heat oil in a skillet. I use Rose's old cast iron pan before cast iron pans were even a "thing." That's right. I use the same goddamn pan that fried young JFK's eggs. Fry each croquette until golden and crispy. Your guests will hardly notice the absence of tuna amidst the golden crunch.

6. Serve:

Present hot and fresh your "Tuna" Croquettes with a twinkle in your eye. As guests marvel at the delightful golden crunch, distract them with talk of something else. Like cryptocurrency.

And there you have it, Ethel Kennedy's "Tuna" Croquettes!!

Monopoly with Marjorie

Step 1: Taking Turns

In Monopoly, "taking turns" is a fundamental concept where players rotate their opportunities to roll dice, acquire properties, and strategically decimate their opponents' bank accounts. This happens in a clockwise fashion around the board, which is just a fancy way of saying "to the right." This tradition prevents the chaos of everyone shouting, "I'm next!" simultaneously, which could frighten pets and small children.

Each player's turn is a thrilling cycle of rolling dice, moving a token (that's the little metal figure that represents you on the board—more on that later), and interacting with squares on the board. These interactions might include buying properties, paying rent, or landing on spaces that require you to draw cards that could either be a ticket to a luxury hotel stay or a devastating tax bill.

Remember, it's important to wait your turn, as tempting as it might be to launch your newly acquired cannon token across the board prematurely. In Monopoly, patience is not just a virtue; it's a requirement, unless you want to be silently judged by your fellow players and potentially the family pet.

Step 2: Adding the Two Numbers on the Dice

Now, this might get a bit complex, so hold onto your top hat (one of the potential tokens you might be navigating). When you roll the dice in Monopoly, you're not just tossing random numbers; you're setting your fate with a pair of six-sided objects known as "dice." Each die has faces numbered from one to six. Your mission, should you choose to accept it, is to roll these dice and add the numbers that land face up. Shocking, I know!

Let's break it down: If you roll a four on the first die and a three on the second, you will need to summon your best math skills to add these together. Using advanced calculations, we find that four plus three equals—wait for it—seven! That's right, you now move your token seven spaces forward.

This process of adding is crucial because it determines how quickly you move around the board, sweeping up properties or tumbling into financial ruin. It's the kind of heart-pounding action that can only be found in a board game that simulates real estate and banking.

Step 3: How Money Works

In the high-stakes world of Monopoly, money isn't just pieces of paper; it's the very lifeblood of your empire. Here's a rundown on this wildly intricate concept: You start with a set amount of "Monopoly money," which is absolutely worthless outside of this game context, so don't try using it at your local grocery store.

As you whirl around the board, you'll spend this money acquiring properties, building houses and hotels, and occasionally handing it over to other players for landing on their upgraded properties. Each time you pass "GO," the Bank (a merciless, non-FDIC insured institution run by whoever was duped into being the banker) grants you $200. Think of it as a tiny, benevolent government stimulus package for your tireless circling.

Money in Monopoly can also disappear faster than dignity at a House of Representatives session. You'll need to manage it wisely, deciding when to invest in properties or save for the inevitable fees from landing on spaces like "Income Tax" or "Jail."

Step 4: I Don't Know Why There is No Georgia—Don't Take it Personally

Ah, the ever-bewildering mystery of why there's no Georgia on the Monopoly board. If you've ever wondered why you can purchase properties in Illinois or Indiana but not in the peachy state of Georgia, you're not alone. It's a question that baffles scholars and casual players alike, akin to pondering why we park on driveways and drive on parkways.

Monopoly's selection of properties is based on the streets of Atlantic City, New Jersey, not a comprehensive map of the U.S. So, while it may seem like a grave oversight or a personal slight against all things Georgian, rest assured, it's merely a quirk of the game's historic design.

Do not despair or take to the streets in protest just yet. The lack of Georgia is not an indictment of its worth or a commentary on its real estate market. Instead, it's a chance to embrace Atlantic City's charm, even if it means forgoing the chance to slap a hotel on Atlanta.

So, when you roll the dice and navigate the bustling avenues of your Monopoly board, remember: every state has its merits, but not every state can make it onto the board. It's not personal—it's just business, Monopoly business. Embrace the mystery, enjoy the game, and who knows? Maybe you'll start a house rule where "Passing Go" means taking a virtual trip through Savannah or Athens, celebrating Georgia in spirit if not in deed.

Brett Kavanaugh Remembers... (Which is a Euphemism for, Brett Kavanaugh Pieces Together Events from Evenings About Which He Has No Recollection)

Went to play trivia with my dad at an applebees . Sat at the bar with him and somehow did about 8 shots of rumple minze on top of the beers we drank that night. Racked up a $140 bar tab that I insisted on paying for . Spent the night back at my parents house in my old room . Woke up covered in piss and realized it was a Thursday morning and I had to go to work . Jumped in the shower and balled up the sheets and dirty clothes in a hamper . Probably still drunk, made my way to work and get a text from my mom " did you get sick last night? " responded " kind of , that's piss. Don't touch the hamper I'll be back after work ." Forever referred to as the " blacking out in the neighborhood night ." Ughhh. Realize now the bartender was seekingrevenge on behalf of the Clintons.

Tried to take a shit. Woke up hours later with my pants around my ankles, on the floor. Everything including the floor, my clothes, and the walls were smeared in crap.

I was thrown out of Denny's by a manager seeking revenge on behalf of the Clintons, pissed on 2 of the 3 guys I was hanging out with while we were in a huddle. They chased me back to the apartment with their dicks out trying to piss on me. Managed not to get pissed on. Woke up in my friend's hall with no clothes, a towel over me in a fashion of a sheet being draped over a dead body. Couldn't find clothes so I sobered up and drove home. In front of a high school band I pulled over and vomited out of my door and shit myself at the same time.

Once I drank an entire fifth of Jägermeister in one sitting. This was at a

Christmas party in college. I literally sat down and did not stand back up until the last drop was consumed, which took a little over an hour (I don't remember getting up). I time traveled 8 hours into the future with no recollection of events that took place. However, I gathered some stories from friends to account for my then broken foot, scraped up face and torso, and bruises all over. The bruises were mostly from falling down two flights of stairs after my friend wouldn't let me in her room because I was scaring her friends. The scratches were mostly from attempting to tackle a tree. A teammate told me that he saw me running full-speed, by myself, at 1am, through the courtyard and intentionally layout into a medium sized tree. He said I just laid there for a solid 5 minutes, and when I finally came to I got up and sprinted away. The broken foot was from kicking the bumper of a car. A friend in town for the weekend said he found me wandering campus solo at around 4am. I'm taking him back to my dorm when I figured it'd be a good idea to run on top of the cars lined up in the parking lot. After jumping about 4 cars or so I finally misstepped and fell. I was so pissed off that I had fallen that I got up and kicked the bumper seemingly as hard as I could. Not a good idea. Those things are designed to sustain impacts. I must say that it was probably the scariest thing I've ever woken up to, not knowing why I was in so much pain, covered in dirt with leaves coming out of my pants and shoes (besides that one time I woke up in jail with no memory of being arrested). Jager and I just don't get along; I realize now that Jagermeister is just seeking revenge on behalf of the Clintons.

I was so drunk I gave the cab the wrong address when I was trying to get home from the bar. He ended up dropped me off like a mile away from where I lived. I walked around trying to get my bearings and slipped on the ice, re-breaking the frames of my glasses and hurting my knee. Eventually I reached what I thought was my entrance to my apartment and tried to get in, but none of my keys worked. I smoked a cigarette and tried calling my roommate, but he didn't pick up. I looked for my car on the street and realized it was not there, I must be at the wrong place. A few minutes later I see a cop car driving up and they stop right in front of me. They ask, "Do you know where you are?" And I said something along the lines of, "Honestly, officers, I'm really drunk. Can you please give me a ride home?" They looked at each other and kind of laughed and one of them said, "I've been there before man. Let me see your ID so I can run your information real quick." I gave them my ID and got in the back seat. I explained more about what happened as they ran my name on their computer. I came up clean, so they decided to give me a ride home. On the way there we talked more, but the best part was when we got close and I told them it's a pain in the ass to get to because of one-way streets and the one driving, looks back and says, "Are you kidding? Look at who you're talking to." He then flashed his lights and went down the wrong way of a one-way street. They dropped me off and told me to stay safe. People talk about white privilege? I earned that ride home.

Long story short I puked on my living room carpet with a house full of guests at about 9pm....on the day of my wife's birthday party. Everybody left after that. They all went to a birthday party thrown by the Clintons.

In high school I took a bottle of vodka form my parents then went to Denny's with my best friend. I remember getting a table, that's it. So, they tell me that I jacked off under the table and moaned so loudly that the waitress had to come to the table and tell me to keep me quiet. Then I went to the bathroom, and fell asleep on the toilet. My best friend had to come get me, He had to help me get my pants up. And I suppose they got me home eventually. Yeah, I missed like 10 hours of my night that night. This whole time, my best friend was hired by the Clintons to seek revenge on their behalf.

On Christmas Eve when I was like 18 I drank double shots of vodka with my grandpa and threw up in my dad's car on the way back home lol. My grandpa was seeking revenge on behalf of the Clintons.

Coming Soon from Reese & Gary

Look for these forthcoming releases, part of Humorist Books's heralded "How to Tell if Someone..." series, wherever you buy books:

"Of Child Prodigies & Churchy Predators: How to Tell if Someone is Haley Joel Osment or Joel Osteen"

Has this ever happened to you: you're out and about and you bump into a familiar face so you walk up to his table or stop im on the sidewalk or sidle up to him on the dance floor and say, "you were great in 'The Sixth Sense'," and wait for a fist bump that never comes and as you walk or sidle away you realize that who you were thought was Haley Joel Osment was really Joel Osteen!!

It's the worst. Well with our new forthcoming book "How to Tell if Someone Is Haley Joel Osment or Joel Osteen: A Guide to Telling the Difference Between Haley Joel Osment and Joel Osteen," this will never happen to you again.

Included are chapters like:

1. "Prodigy or Predator? (Hint: Haley Joel Osment is the Prodigy and Joel Osteen is the Predator)"

2. "M. Night Shyamalan or Malachi 3:10: One Directs Moving Pictures and One is Used to Distort Scripture"

3. "'I See Dead People' versus 'God wants us to prosper financially, to have plenty of money, to fulfill the destiny He has laid out for us': Both are Fiction"

4. "Pay It Forward and By Forward I Mean To Me, Joel Scott Osteen"

"How You Like Them Apples: And How You Like to Tell if Someone is Matt Damon or Jesse Plemons"

Still talking to Jesse Plemons's people on this one. He's being difficult and wants us to call the book "Stop Calling Me Fat Matt Damon: The Jesse Plemons Story" and we're all like "But Jesse Plemons that's not the format" and well, we can't really tell you all the negotiations because of the lawyers and yada yada yada.

ACKNOWLEDGEMENTS

Gary thanks Brian Boone, Marty Dundics, and everyone at Humorist Books for their hard work and unwavering support. Thanks to everyone who can make us laugh at the absurdity that is politics in 2024 but also thanks to everyone who does what they do to protect our right (for now) to laugh and even bigger thanks to everyone helping those who can only cry. Thanks also to my best friend and co-author Reese for his astonishingly good humor, for picking the best &^$%ing fonts, and for writing everything with which you have taken issue. Finally, thanks to Malgosza Stankewicz Zawadzki, Ho Chi Minh, Deborah Chantel, and Moshkan Bedoya.

Reese would like to thank the many friends who encouraged him to keep writing whenever he'd say pathetic things like, "No one's gonna read this book." He'd like to shout out Hudson Hill in Denver for providing him coffee, WiFi, and comfort throughout the writing process. He'd like to praise his parents for supporting his decision to major in English (it finally paid off). Finally, he'd like to acknowledge his publishers, Marty Dundics and Brian Boone, and his co-author and best friend Gary, without whom this book would have never happened.

The End

www.ingramcontent.com/pod-product-compliance
Lightning Source LLC
Chambersburg PA
CBHW071329120626
46546CB00002B/498